Smash The Boulder

Eliza Jane Blake

Smash the Boulder

Understanding the autistic brain and promoting positive relationships in the workplace

By Eliza Jane Blake

Smash the Boulder is written by Eliza Jane Blake and published by Awesome Scribblers United.

Copyright © 2024, Eliza Jane Blake.

Without the permission of Eliza Jane Blake, reproducing any part of this publication, in any form, is strictly prohibited.

ISBN: 978-1-0687626-1-1 (print version)

Dedication

I dedicate this book to autistic workers who, like me, struggle in work environments that don't accommodate our needs and where we frequently face rejection and condemnation from a society that misunderstands our traits.

Eliza Jane Blake

Table of Contents

- Dedication v
- Foreword 9
- Why Bother? 12
- The Diversity Train 19
- Autistic Spectrum Disorder (ASD) 29
- It's a Social Thing 38
- Oh Literally! 49
- Bottoms-Up 61
- Looks Deceive 68
- We Grow Too 77
- Can You Sense It? 92
- Calmly Does It 100
- Stress is the Limit 107
- Sick and Tired 122
- That's Dedication 135
- How Hard can it Be? 140
- The Autistic Reality 150
- Level it Up 161
- All Aboard 173
- Thanks for Listening 179
- Acknowledgements 184
- About the Author 186

Eliza Jane Blake

Foreword by the Author

There are a couple of points I'd like to clarify. The first is that while the opinions and interpretations in this book are my own, I've engaged in wider research on the experience of others on the autistic spectrum and much of what I say is based on the common experience, not just my own. I recognise, however, that some will have experienced their lives differently and will hold different views. These differences result from personal life experiences and because of how the spectrum works. Mainly, though, the reason for these differences is that autistic people are individuals with brains as complex as every person with a typical (neurotypical) brain.

Second, I wrote this book to educate about autistic adults, not children. Contrary to the beliefs of many – including the first doctor I consulted on my journey to diagnosis – autistic brains are for life and autistic children grow up to become autistic adults. We grow, learn and make progress just as neurotypical people do – even if the rate of that progress is slower. Behaviours and traits in autistic adults, therefore, can follow a recognisable pattern, but don't always appear the same as autistic children.

I should also point out that I wrote this book to educate about those autistic adults who are without intellectual disability. There's a common misconception that 'Autism' – I loathe that word – is a learning disability. The correct position is that some autistic people have intellectual disabilities just as some neurotypical people have intellectual disabilities, but a lack of intelligence isn't a marker or requirement for an Autistic Spectrum Disorder (ASD) diagnosis. For this reason, there are many autistic people, regardless of whether they know they're autistic, who're struggling in the workplace. Many are under-employed or blocked from advancement in their jobs and many others want to work but find themselves excluded. In both cases, this is usually a consequence of prejudice, or past misinterpretations about the way our brains function.

This book will guide you through the differences between how autistic brains function compared to the neurotypical brain, in an easily understood, but comprehensive way. I would recommend reading chronologically, at least on the initial pass, as each chapter follows from the preceding chapter and ties together as you work through the book.

For autistic people, the consequences of ignorance are too significant to tiptoe around or down-play, so I haven't held back or attempted to sugar-coat anything unsavoury. As you read, I'll ask you to re-think or reframe what you currently believe about social behaviour and the expectations society demands of us all. Few neurotypicals realise that traits they deem undesirable or unacceptable often signify an autistic brain and will attribute those traits to other causes. Acceptance of autistic people involves a big shift in thinking and challenging current beliefs will elicit resistance in some.

Thankfully, most would now agree that it's wrong to condemn homosexuality, but it took time for society to lift its resistance to accepting this truth. The beliefs about autistic traits are just as deeply entrenched and may take time to overcome, but an open mind will help to limit resistance. For what it's worth, there are neurotypical traits that autistic people find just as offensive as neurotypicals find ours, but we need to understand each other to overcome our differences.

Why Bother?

Just for fun, let me paint a picture. Imagine a reality where, many years ago, the moon was partially habitable and a group of humans happily lived upon its surface in an area protected from the glare of the sun. It was a peaceful existence suited to their need for calm, but resources were finite and running low. They desperately clung to the safe and predictable life they enjoyed away from the hustle and bustle favoured by most humans, but inevitably, had to accept their fate and devise a plan to travel to the mother planet, Earth.

They arrived quietly and, following orders, hid in plain sight among the locals. What could go wrong? They looked the same. They sounded the same – nearly. Most could almost get away with it, but there was a problem; a blip in the programming of their brains they hadn't been aware of: they didn't think in the same way as the locals. They'd learnt the language for the country they were to make their home, but time constraints meant they hadn't known so much communication on Earth was non-verbal. They also hadn't known their brains communicated in a style that was different to the locals.

If that wasn't enough, they hadn't anticipated how chaotic their new environment would be or how difficult they would find adjusting to it. The moon had been a quiet place, but by comparison, Earth was harsh, overwhelming and sometimes physically painful for these sensitive souls. They found the difference in lifestyle between the two communities a dramatic culture shock, but there was no going back; the moon couldn't support their existence anymore.

Unfortunately, the natives weren't open to strangers – they didn't trust difference and felt compelled to reject, or even sometimes, destroy anyone who didn't conform to their expectations. Desperate, the autists (or autistics) did what they could to survive. Some could mimic those around them consistently, while others created hard or bolshy exteriors. Some engaged in physical battles to survive and some retreated into themselves; minimising the harm they experienced from living in a hostile environment that wasn't designed for them, but which they had no choice but to accept.

For a while, they survived, with some faring better than others. Some, mainly the younger ones, believed they'd got the pretence off to a tee; they could do this and the locals didn't seem any the wiser. But others struggled and floundered out of their depth with no idea what they were doing wrong. Over time, things could only get worse for them, and those who'd initially faked with ease found it became harder as they got older.

Greater age into adulthood brought greater responsibility and more stress. The autists' once robust health showed cracks. Many of those who'd struggled couldn't continue anymore; the hostility from the locals had become too much to bear and the personal cost of survival too much to manage.

The locals had their customs, social expectations and style of communicating. They believed that anyone with an intelligent brain could understand their ways and that those who spoke in the same language should also be able to communicate in their style. They believed that the things they found instinctive should be instinctive to everyone; that their normal was the way for all.

The locals didn't know that some people had brains that were wired to process information and communicate in a different style. Based on their own experience, they believed that those who said things they didn't like, in a way they didn't like, were being rude and needed to learn the error of their ways. They believed in the power of punishment and collectively they had immense strength. They wouldn't tolerate non-compliance. The offensive people would learn or pay the price for their rudeness.

Research shows that autistic people are more likely to end their life by suicide than neurotypical people. We're more likely to be unemployed or under-employed. We're more

Smash The Boulder

likely to find ourselves subjected to disciplinary procedures in the workplace and our ability to do our job is rarely the reason. Most often, our managers have deemed us a poor fit in a social sense or believe that we have an attitude problem, according to neurotypical standards. If we have a job, we're more likely to be financially poorer and blocked from progressing within the organisation.

Social isolation is common for autistic people and not limited to the workplace. Autistic people are also more likely to be manipulated by others. Too often, people adopt a buyer beware attitude towards life, believing this to be a dog-eat-dog world, and often, even when they know someone lacks the awareness to protect themself, will gleefully take advantage, just because they can. It's the people who take this stance that create and perpetuate a standard that lacks integrity.

In the western world, not so long ago, women were second to men. Skin colour was a massive barrier to equal treatment and being gay wasn't just frowned upon, it was criminal. Decent people faced incarceration simply for being different. Many argue that prejudice in these areas still exists, but we've made progress, even if there's still a way to go. Change is necessary. It's also a fact of life, but sometimes it needs a nudge in the right direction. Sometimes, it needs much more than a nudge.

When there's a mountain to climb to elicit change for oppressed people, only tenacity, audacity and willing supporters will beat the inevitable resistance. For most minority groups, the change is already happening and has been for a while, but for autistic people, the required change is barely off the starting blocks. The mountain looms large ahead of us, and some autistic people accept the insistent view of the majority who believe that our brains are faulty, and therefore substandard.

Prejudgement, ignorance, and a reluctance to open closed minds are barriers that people now recognise and are dismantling to the benefit of many minority groups, but they still prevail, mainly unchallenged, in the arena of neurodiversity. The way autistic and other neurodivergent people find themselves prevented from flourishing in the modern workplace has broad consequences for them, but nothing will change without an acknowledgment and willingness to correct it. Change must happen, but it won't unless we're all open to learning about our differences and recognising them for what they really are when we see them.

I believe autistic brains represent a neurotype rather than a spectrum disorder and I'm not alone in thinking this, but being diagnosed autistic, and therefore having a recognised disability, is what protects all autists with a diagnosis in the current climate of ignorance. It doesn't, however, help those without a diagnosis and labelling us disabled encourages minds to remain closed. To some, it perpetuates a derogatory belief that we're substandard, faulty and not part of mainstream society; only tolerated and accommodated out of obligation.

A lifetime of condemnation, criticism, ridicule and contempt preceded the diagnosis of ASD that has enabled me to make some sense of my life experiences; to understand why, despite doing well at school, my working life has been one disaster after another, why relationships and friendships are best left to other people, and why solitude is always a sanctuary.

Smash The Boulder

My family drilled into me from an early age that my struggles and problems were my doing because I wasn't trying hard enough. There was no help or support, just frowning, scowling, mocking belittlements and comments that I should know better by now. My research has revealed that I'm far from alone in this experience.

I've lived a life riddled with misunderstandings and demands from others who've expected me to change and be someone that I'm not, with punishments thrown at me for every perceived failure to meet those expectations and if you're thinking I'm saying all of this out of self-pity, you're wrong. I'm saying this because my experience isn't unique. Autistic people find themselves expected to live inauthentic lives because most people don't recognise autistic traits when they see them. Many people have other names to describe us, and some aren't shy about using them.

People assume rudeness where none exists. They assume explanations for what they see and hear without doubting the validity of their assumptions. They assume a lack of intelligence where intelligence may be in abundance, and they assume the right to judge and punish with impunity.

My use of the word assume is no accident; it represents a core difference between people born of the standard neurotype and those of the detail-driven autistic neurotype. Neurotypical assumptions are plentiful and cause problems when observed through an autistic lens. The problem is that these assumptions aren't being made on a like-for-like basis. Neurotypical people just believe they are. Because autistic brains work so differently, the likelihood of neurotypical assumptions being accurate is rather thin, but the harm caused to us by inaccurate assumptions is, sadly, significant.

Eliza Jane Blake

It's often the assumption that autistic people are just rude neurotypicals (unless we have a piece of paper saying otherwise) that leads to us being expected to live our lives with our comfort zones stretched to a point that ultimately results in illness, or at the very least, a break-down in the ability to pretend to be someone that we're not.

Faking our personalities to make us more acceptable to neurotypicals is called autistic masking, and for us, the inevitable consequence is burnout. Masking isn't unique to autistic people. Most people wear a mask every time they attend a job interview, but for us it's essential to our survival on a day-to-day basis and always entails a denial and burial of our true natures in public.

Unfortunately, the price we pay for acceptance is high – too high. If we can't mask successfully, the judgements, contempt and constant assault on our self-esteem are bad enough, but that's before we even consider the financial ramifications of trying to exist in a world that is unaccommodating and unforgiving.

Now is the time for that change. Awareness of diversity and the importance of inclusion is growing every day and working well for most minority groups, but unwittingly, it can negatively affect neurodivergent people. This book endeavours to correct this situation and help create a reality where autistic, and other neurodivergent groups, can feel safe living authentic lives.

The Diversity Train

In the modern workplace, managers often encourage employees to bring their true selves to work. They actively encourage people to be confident about doing this and their motives are honourable, but while this is a great idea in principle and works well with the minority groups who've already fought and gained traction in their battle for equality, it's a dangerous invitation to extend to those with different brain function.

Most people don't recognise the traits of neurodivergent people, or at least, they don't recognise them for what they are. My last two employed positions encouraged staff to bring their true selves to work, but without first training themselves or their existing staff to recognise neurodivergence, least of all understand it. For other minority groups, integration, cooperation and acceptance at work is commonplace, but because awareness about neurodivergence is still in the stalls, this is a big problem.

The western world accepts it's inappropriate to treat a physically disabled person as an inconvenience because their wheelchair is big, bulky and in other people's way. It's also not acceptable to expect gay people to put themselves into aversion therapy to cure them of their difference. Yet, at the time of writing, many employers submit potential recruits to an appraisal by questionnaire, designed to identify people with undesirable personality traits – traits that are often found in the neurodivergent community.

It's also true that many employers subject neurodivergent workers to disciplinary procedures, or performance measures and oust them from jobs in which they perform well, just because they don't perceive that person as a good fit in a social sense – often based upon neurotypical expectations that neurodivergent people aren't wired to meet. This is blatant discrimination towards autistic and other neurodivergent people, but most employers either haven't realised this yet, or are reluctant to acknowledge it. Most companies haven't recognised that it's appropriate to update their HR (Human Resources) policies or create neurodivergent-friendly policies that allow for alternate neurotypes.

It's a significant step in the right direction that enlightened employers are encouraging employees to bring their true selves to work, but a lot more needs to be done to understand neurodiversity before making such blanket invitations. Inviting people who've worn a mask their whole lives to remove that mask not only leaves them feeling more exposed than they've ever felt before, but because of the prevailing

Smash The Boulder

ignorance, they're being invited to face a metaphorical firing squad.

Understanding must come first. There can be no acceptance or cooperation without it. I have no desire to derail the diversity train or the positive progress we've all been making towards a more inclusive society, but I implore caution. Most people know little about neurodiversity and what they know, or think they know, is often flawed and skewed by stereotypes or relates to children rather than adults.

The biggest problem is that society raises its people to expect neurotypical social standards, and for many autistic people, this is unrealistic. The harm done to us is on a par with the discrimination previously faced by both the gay and black communities. We too have been, and remain, ostracised by a society that accepts the belief that autistic traits are unacceptable, without ever questioning why or knowing that the traits they hate so much even represent a different type of brain function.

We need neurotypical people to recognise what they're seeing for what it really is. Autistic people and others who're neurodivergent deserve a fair crack at life, but that will never happen until society, in particular business owners, managers and everyone who is part of a workforce, recognises that there is more than one neurotype within the human species and willingly meets us half-way. It's not as simple as demanding people stop being bigots and open their minds. The change required is on a monumental level. Only a real concerted effort to train and educate on a massive scale will undo the damage caused to autistic people by past ignorance.

Eliza Jane Blake

Everybody knows or has met someone who's neurodivergent, even if they don't realise it. Statistically, autists represent at least 1% of the population. I believe 1.5% is closer at the time of writing. The actual position is probably higher than that, and even then, the figures don't include those who essentially have an autistic brain, but without sufficient struggles to warrant a diagnosis. I'm certain my son has an autistic brain, but unlike me, he doesn't have regulation problems. For this reason alone, his neurotype isn't problematic for him to the same extent as it is for me and many others.

When I had my initial assessment with the National Health Service (NHS) in January 2019, I was told that full testing would be a wait of between ten months and a year. When we entered lockdown in March 2020, fourteen months later, I was still waiting. In fact, I was to wait three years to receive my diagnosis with a caveat that there would be a delay for the full report, with pressures on the service being cited as the reason for the delay. A clinical psychologist told me they had 5,500 people on the waiting list for the assessment and that's just in one county. Not country, county!

This matters to us because three years is a long time to wait for confirmation that we're not imagining a cause for difficulties that runs much deeper than everyone assumes; particularly when the reason for those struggles is biological, not behavioural. When an autistic person tries to exist in a workplace that doesn't recognise different neurotypes, the lack of a diagnosis puts that person at risk of disciplinary procedures and potentially losing their job, or even their home, so time is crucial.

Smash The Boulder

There are many autistic people caught in this situation and there are a lot of autistic people across the world. At 1% of the population, that would still be 1 in 100 in a UK population of approximately 67.8 million people. Consider an estimation of the world's population being 8.1 billion and 1% is therefore 81 million people. That's a lot of autists. In fact, it's on a par with the size of Germany's population.

The number of autistic people is significant. Our traits are just misinterpreted. Incidentally, much of what you read in this book also applies to those with Attention-Deficit-Hyperactivity-Disorder (ADHD) a neurotype recognised to represent closer to 3-4% of the population. The difference between the two is that while the autistic brain is mainly a social disability because of communication and information processing differences; ADHD is predominantly a disability of executive function, which can have social implications as a consequence. But I can't help wondering if the prevalence of autistic brains is on a par with ADHD, just less recognised because many autistic children are less likely to be noticed in the classroom.

So, I'll do my best to de-bunk the myths and clarify the truth because far too many autists, myself included, are good people routinely condemned and side-lined in a working world that doesn't understand us when we have so much to offer. I don't want our young people with autistic brains to experience the world of work in the same way that my generation has; to reach a point where they feel like they're walking on eggshells every day in case they unintentionally offend someone and fear for the punishment that will inevitably follow.

Eliza Jane Blake

Today's young who have a diagnosis (and many still won't) often have access to support while they remain in education, but the consideration and understanding they rely upon disappears when they go out into the world of work. There's so much ground to cover to educate society and bring about a tangible understanding of how autistic brains function and how autistic people experience the world around them. What I've learnt since embarking on my journey to diagnosis and beyond is that those who have an official diagnosis, regardless of their age, rarely declare it to their current or prospective employers. They've discovered that the diagnosis itself is a means to discriminate against them, or just as bad, the lack of understanding among their managers and co-workers about the reality of how their brains function, mean they face the same level of hostility and distrust as those who've never received a diagnosis.

For most of us, having a diagnosis helps us little unless our employers, managers and co-workers willingly help to create environments that minimise the harm a neurotypical working environment can unwittingly cause. More important, what this entails is usually much easier and unobtrusive than you might imagine. The larger the employer, the greater the likelihood of the organisation having a diversity policy. Neurodivergent people, however, differ from other minority groups in that the tolerance and understanding needed from those around them is on a level not seen since the others' fights for equality were in their infancy.

Beliefs about what makes a person acceptable in society are deeply entrenched and many will resist changing them. The lack of education in our communities almost guarantees a reluctance or outright refusal to accommodate us in many businesses – especially small businesses. Most people simply don't recognise different brain function when they encounter it and are quick to treat those who're different with contempt, satisfied in their own minds that we deserve the treatment we're receiving, because we need to learn or should know better.

Most people in a workplace setting can recognise minority groups and act appropriately, but because neurodivergence relates to brain function, this creates a unique problem. When people encounter a person with different brain chemistry, they don't realise they're bullying or being unfair to someone with a recognised disability. They 'know' that people who come across like us deserve to be punished and they assume the right to do exactly that. But our difference isn't about behaviour and there's no choice in being born autistic.

Unfortunately, smaller or unenlightened employers have no compulsion to accommodate people who're different and will shamelessly discriminate against those who declare a neurological disability. It's easy to recognise that this is probably because it requires everybody within an organisation to make a conscious effort and people imagine, incorrectly, that the effort required is significant.

People don't want anyone in their world who makes them feel uncomfortable. Even in the workplace, they want an environment where everybody is compatible socially and when they talk about people skills, what they really mean is, neurotypical people skills. Autistic people often feel like the alien in the office when neurotypicals make us feel uncomfortable, so it cuts both ways, but doesn't justify our exclusion, particularly if the organisation proclaims to advocate inclusivity.

Think about that. What's the alternative? Segregated employments with neurotypical workers in one building and autistic in another? Not so long ago, some countries had separate public bars for black people, and gay people found themselves segregated from the rest of society by incarceration. Is segregation appropriate? In what way is rejecting candidates, or dismissing autistic employees based on perceived undesirable traits, not already segregation in action?

Bringing us all together, however, isn't as simple as telling everybody to stop treating autistic people as if they're bad people, because without an understanding of why the differences exist, or perhaps more accurately what they mean, we can't hope to change the currently entrenched views that are held by most people.

There are many who believe they don't mistreat others, but that's because they believe people who have autistic traits deserve the punishments meted out to them. They don't realise the expected standards of their own neurotype limit their beliefs about how people should behave. There's no awareness of neurological difference and this leads to intolerance; a resistance to difference that reflects the history of our society. The time is overdue for a reappraisal.

Unfortunately, when people think the effort required to tackle this inequality is too much, they simply obstruct such undesirables from gaining entry to the workplace. So, autists (who know they're autistic) find themselves caught in a trap. If they declare their disability from the outset, they'll most often not get past the interview stage, but if they don't declare their disability, the employer will resist working with them to make any reasonable adjustments after the fact, and by reasonable adjustments, I don't mean favourable treatment.

The worst scenario is when an autist declares their diagnosis and it seems to be accepted, but then punishment and disciplinary action follow because management hasn't understood what the diagnosis means. It's unlikely company policies will reflect accommodations for neurodivergent employees, so even if managers have a basic knowledge, they find themselves in a dilemma about how to proceed.

Autistic people have much to offer and contribute to the workplace, and they should have as much right to work as everybody else, but all too often those who work, find themselves held back by a culture that insists on placing more worth on soft skills than expertise and practical ability. The emphasis is shamelessly skewed towards that in which neurotypical people naturally excel. Unfortunately, this is at the expense of those who aren't neurotypical.

We can, though, dismantle the obstruction barring autistic opportunity. Autistic people are human beings, entitled to the same opportunities and level of respect as everybody else. Most people like to believe they're decent and, fortunately, decency is all we need to achieve equality for autistic people.

We're capable, industrious, and dedicated when given the opportunity. This is a mutual benefit to be embraced. Not only would the autistic population succeed without restraint, but by learning about us rather than shunning us, neurotypical people may recognise that much of what they find offensive about us isn't personal and never was.

There's a moral choice to be made by employers who sell themselves as supportive of diversity. Will they make themselves open and friendly towards autistic people and other neurotypes? If not, will they add a caveat to their diversity policy that excludes different neurotypes? It isn't right, or fair, for companies to claim openness to diversity but then begin disciplinary procedures every time something undesirable, but connected to a person's neurotype, occurs. Obviously, the legal position remains that those with a recognised neurological disability have protection from discrimination, but managers who lack understanding or tolerance often choose to ignore this or don't realise the behaviour they're punishing is a consequence of a person's neurotype or disability.

Then there are those autists who've never undergone assessment but are just as autistic as the rest of us – they just can't prove it. Where is their protection from discrimination and exile? Many autistic people, especially in the thirty plus age group, find themselves in this position. I hope that education within the workplace will enable more people to recognise those with an autistic brain, particularly those who've had no help or support thus far, but to achieve this we need to understand what ASD is and we need to identify how people can recognise it.

Autistic Spectrum Disorder (ASD)

What does it mean to be autistic and what do you know about it? Do you think it's primarily a behavioural or intellectual disability? Does your mind conjure a picture of a screaming child, a silent child, or a studious one? What does an autistic person look like? How would you know if you were standing next to one? Most people aren't aware that ASD is mainly a social difference. Most people, unless they're autistic, have autistic family members, or are trained professionals, can't recognise the traits and know little about what it means to have an autistic brain.

What most people think they know is usually a product of what they've seen in films or is based entirely upon assumption. So, if not a screaming child, most neurotypicals will conjure the image of a non-speaking person, or an intellectually gifted one, but most autistic people don't fit these descriptions.

To be autistic is to have a brain with complex traits, known collectively as the spectrum, but people commonly misunderstand what the spectrum is. Most people imagine the spectrum as a straight-line diagram with severe at one end and mild at the other, but this isn't how it works. Autistic people share identified, recognisable traits, but how they affect us will vary from person to person. This is the spectrum. It isn't possible to consider the traits of any autistic person and point to a place along a straight-line to designate where they fit.

An easy way to visualise the spectrum is to imagine a bar chart with the various traits along the x axis and the height of each tower reflecting affectedness for each trait on the individual. Alternatively, the more common way of depicting the extent by which autistic traits affect each person is with a circle diagram, or a wheel, divided into equal segments to represent each trait and a variable amount of colouring within each segment to reflect the affectedness. The key detail is that all autistic people are equally autistic, just as all neurotypical people are equally neurotypical. For all of us, our personal differences exist within the spectrum of traits. We're all individuals.

However, for anyone to receive a diagnosis, the consequence to their life is significant. Therefore, society automatically recognises anyone who receives a diagnosis as disabled. It's entirely possible to have an autistic brain and not need a diagnosis; it's the personal consequence while living in a neurotypical world that matters.

Smash The Boulder

The commonalities that affect the entire spectrum show in ways that require different degrees of support. Those who don't have learning difficulties, however, are no less in need of support while the current level of ignorance and intolerance persists. Some autists need twenty-four-hour care, while others can live independently, but in some ways, those who don't have learning difficulties struggle the most simply because they rarely receive the support or recognition they need.

I've said this knowing I've just stirred up many people who're now demanding to know how I can say such a thing. The clearly disabled, those who can't look after themselves, obviously need more help. Well, yes, of course they do, but most autistic people who need twenty-four-hour care are already getting the help they need. They're rarely responsible for the costs involved in keeping a roof over their heads and aren't trying to survive in the world of work. Whereas those without intellectual impairment are, and it's for those people, that I'm writing this book. I'm advocating for the over-looked, diminished, forgotten and dismissed.

People are more accommodating and willing to help others when they can see a visible impairment. Most autistic people, without intellectual difficulties, have an invisible difference. Outwardly, we look like everybody else and because we're intelligent, this leads to the assumption that we're just bad neurotypicals rather than disabled or having a different neurotype. So, the type of support an autist may need varies and for many autistic people, awareness, tolerance and acceptance would be enough. Understanding about the autistic neurotype, however, hasn't been available to the wider community and because of this, society misinterprets our traits and punishes us instead.

There's a common misconception that people who're intelligent should automatically be capable of communicating in the neurotypical way, but different neurotypes have their own way of communicating, and it's this that leads neurotypicals to punish us so often.

Having autistic brain function means that a person thinks, processes information, and communicates differently from the majority. What most consider a behavioural disorder in children is nothing of the sort. What neurotypicals see in autistic children is a consequence of different brain chemistry. It's because of how autistic children react to their surroundings that we're all assumed to be loud, disruptive and problematic, but any such behaviour is a response to a chaotic world that's overwhelming or harming us, regardless of our age. In truth, if autists ruled the world, everybody's life would be so calm and controlled, neurotypicals wouldn't know what to do with themselves without all the chaos.

The behaviour neurotypicals consider poor or uncontrolled, is a desperate form of communication; an acute need for something to change because that person is suffering. It's a distress call that requires action to remove or reduce the source of the upset, but often the response is punishment instead. Most people think the source of the upset shouldn't be upsetting and that the autist is being melodramatic. Instead of empathy, therefore, we receive contempt.

Autistic brains are more stimulated than neurotypical brains. Our brains don't stop and always need to be doing or thinking about something. We find it very difficult to switch off or to sit still without something else to concentrate on, and it's because of this greater stimulation that our brains can become overwhelmed by various triggers; triggers that have no effect on neurotypicals. When this happens, we need calm and order bringing to our environment, either by removing the source of distress, or by removing ourselves.

Unfortunately, what we usually get at these times is an increase of whatever is distressing us, because neurotypicals believe we need to learn to tolerate 'what is' and will ramp up the source of the upset to bring home what we need to learn. By doing this, they increase the suffering and perceived undesirable behaviour, rather than reducing it.

It's a harmful approach and, if you noticed, I said that it's our brain that becomes overwhelmed, not the person. There's a truth to this that most neurotypicals don't recognise or will refuse to accept, despite society currently classifying our neurotype as a disability. Indeed, there are autistic people who reject it because neurotypicals have trained them to take total responsibility for their reactions and some appear to have been able to do so.

But when we consider the nature of the spectrum and how we're all affected to different degrees across the array of traits, it isn't reasonable for any person, neurotypical or autistic, to declare what any autistic person should be capable of. So, yes, there's sometimes an element of being out of control, but that needs to be acknowledged and approached in the right way. Bully-boy tactics and insisting we exert a level of control over our reactions that's on a par with neurotypicals, is unfair, unrealistic and often achieves little.

I'm not saying that autists have no responsibility, I'm saying that it's impossible to say how capable any autist can be of meeting that responsibility because it's a variable; both on a personal level and from day-to-day. It's also true that the greater the demands made upon us, the greater the stress created and the greater the likelihood of overwhelm occurring. A gentle approach achieves far more. The autist and everyone around them can learn to navigate those triggers in an environment that's open to trial and error rather than trying to control the autist with an iron rod.

In truth, the situations that cause us to become overwhelmed are usually easily avoidable by making simple efforts to adjust our exposure to certain triggers. But we need neurotypical cooperation to make this a reality. Trying to force our brains to comply with neurotypical social etiquette is on a par with expecting a one-armed person to grow another arm so they'll be like everyone else.

I know little about brain biology, but from what I can understand, there are several areas of autistic brains that function differently to neurotypical brains, and they're all involved in social interaction and communication.

Autistic brains develop inconsistently, so an autist's development may show advancement in some areas but lag in others. As I mentioned before, the spectrum recognises the commonalities between autistic people and the varying degrees of affectedness. We need society to recognise, however, that neurotypical needs are no more important than ours. We all matter. There's no justification for dismissing autistic needs as irrelevant or inconvenient just because the limitations of the neurotypical experience mean they don't understand why they matter. Reasonable adjustments in the workplace are exactly that.

Smash The Boulder

There are some who believe that society should find a cure to eradicate the autistic neurotype, and where the reason is to remove the effect on those who can't care for themselves, I can understand why people would want to do this as a positive step towards alleviating the distress some autists experience. Unfortunately, however, there are just as many neurotypicals who want to see a cure for their own benefit; to make their own lives easier and more comfortable at the expense of us.

This neurotypical desire for a cure creates conflict between them and the autistic community because most autistic people don't want one. We are who we are and how we are is normal to us. Not to mention that we can see the drawbacks of neurotypical brain function and prefer our own. The desire to eradicate our neurotype smacks of the same cleansing that motivated the Nazis. It's a minority of autistic people who need twenty-four-hour care, just as it's a minority of neurotypical people who need twenty-four-hour care. Researchers established the idea of the spectrum a few years ago in response to the realisation there was a much broader scope to the autistic brain than previously believed. The suffering of a few doesn't justify the eradication of an entire neurotype.

Yes, some autistic people struggle more than others and may need more direct help from other people. I hope, for their sake, that a reduction in any suffering is achievable. However, autists are not pointless people. We don't lack intelligence or purpose. Most autistic people's desire for acceptance by society shows this regardless of whether we can speak or rely upon technology to assist us. Why shouldn't we want to survive? Not only are we not bad people, but we'd also be a lot more relaxed and comfortable within our own skins and around everyone else, if we weren't constantly feeling the stress of walking on eggshells while we try to navigate a world that isn't designed with us in mind and which is intolerant of our differences.

There's more than one operating system available to human brains. There is, and always has been, more than one way to process information and communicate with the world. Autists know neurotypicals can find us offensive. My mother drilled into me, as a child, that I must not cause offense! The demand was completely moot because I don't have a neurotypical brain and how I communicate is instinctive to me, just as the way neurotypicals communicate is instinctive to them.

However, what I never understood and which I found unfair was the fact that people subjected me to punishment every time I got it wrong in their eyes, while it never seemed to matter if other people offended me. It was perfectly okay for other people to say and do as they pleased, in ways that I found offensive, but because their dissatisfaction with me was considered understandable, the only person ever punished was me.

Balance is a wonderful thing. Most autists know how wrong we are. How can we not when the world impresses their dissatisfaction upon us on such a regular basis? We must learn to understand the neurotypical way and be just like neurotypicals if we want to be accepted! I shouldn't have to point out how arrogant and self-serving this is, but if we want to coexist without antagonism, it's only fair neurotypicals have the same opportunity to understand us, as they expect us to understand them. Our brains will never operate in the

Smash The Boulder

same way and our communication styles will never be compatible, but awareness can help to eliminate many of the misunderstandings that plague us. We're all social people, even if it doesn't feel that way. We just do it differently.

It's a Social Thing

So, being autistic is predominantly a social difference. Looking at both verbal and non-verbal communication is a good starting point to understand how.

Neurotypicals love to talk. No, they need to talk. It doesn't matter what the subject is, so long as they're interacting with someone, they feel connected and energised. But for us, small talk can be excruciatingly uncomfortable. We can talk about specific subjects easily and readily, especially if it's of particular interest, but mundane, irrelevant nonsense, which is how autistic people see small talk, is just too difficult, especially if we don't know someone and don't know if it's safe to relax in their company. We don't need to talk to people in this way, but society expects it from us.

Silence isn't uncomfortable for autists, especially if we're comfortable in the presence of those in the room, but neurotypicals often take our silence as a personal rejection of them when this isn't the case. It takes time for us to reach the point of being comfortable with someone. We can be nervous because others judge us and find us wanting so often. We need to know we can trust someone before we can relax with them, secure that they won't use what many perceive as awkwardness or a lack of neurotypical social skills, against us. It's often the expectation of negative judgements that results in the awkwardness and so the dance comes full circle.

Most neurotypicals can't appreciate how stressful social interaction can be for autistic people, because while neurotypicals find it energising, we find it draining. The way neurotypicals communicate isn't instinctive to us as it is to them and, therefore, takes a huge mental effort on our part, to achieve. Some of us find it impossible and others find they can only do it for so long before it becomes too much.

You may have heard that autistic people lack social skills, but I dispute this accusation. Autists may lack neurotypical social skills, but we don't lack autistic social skills. We can speak passionately on topics that are genuinely interesting to us, often to the point of talking too much, but the topic must hold our interest.

Often considered introverted, just as many autists wouldn't consider themselves to be so. Many undiagnosed autists wrongly conclude that they're shy when they're just wary of being misunderstood and judged. The problem is that many of the extraverted autists have had their wings clipped and are wary of getting it wrong. Others may have received a diagnosis when they were young and be more confident because neurotypicals trained them in how to appear neurotypical. This may seem like a good thing, but it isn't. For most of us, though, it's the fear of being misunderstood, negatively judged and punished that creates the visible awkwardness.

This nervousness when we're in social settings, regardless of whether an autist is introverted or extraverted, can often lead to total withdrawal out of fear of humiliation or rejection. Just the knowledge that past encounters haven't gone well, without understanding why, can lead to nervousness in the company of others. This then leads to accusations of being anti-social, when our aim was only to protect ourselves from the onslaught of criticism, scowling, frowning and the inevitable silent treatment that usually follows such judgements.

Hostility is a reality we encounter regularly, whether it takes the form of silent treatment, loud mocking, or ridiculing belittlements. Is it any wonder we choose withdrawal? The insistence of neurotypicals that we should try harder to be the same as them is unhelpful and again, geared towards their need to uphold the rules and expectations that suit their own social communication style. But because we're often branded anti-social, we can end up trying too hard to meet neurotypical social expectations, resulting in over-friendliness instead.

We don't do this on purpose, but it reflects the reality that while neurotypical standards of socialising are instinctive to them, we're effectively wearing blindfolds and stumbling around in the dark, trying to bluff our way through a minefield without a map to guide us. This is a situation that is often made worse by a limited ability to read faces. We can see obvious hostility, for example, but neurotypicals often mask their true, unpleasant feelings. Or rather, I'm told, will communicate the feeling in more subtle ways. Autists often struggle to read faces, to varying degrees, and will miss neurotypical social cues. Unless others are clear to us about their thoughts and feelings, autists are often unsure about how to respond, or how our efforts to respond are being received.

Some people claim that non-verbal communication accounts for as much as ninety-three per cent of the information humans read in others. Autists struggle with non-verbal communication, but neurotypicals expect us to understand it, as they do. During the assessment that led to my diagnosis, this was the test I struggled with the most. I started believing the assessors were taking the mickey out of me because I found it so difficult. It was impossible.

The assessors presented me with a pair of eyes and four emotions to choose from to best describe what the owner of the eyes was feeling. I could usually rule out a couple, but then had no clue what I was supposed to be seeing in the other two. Eventually, I picked multiple-choice answers at random because I simply couldn't do it. I hadn't been aware this was something that marked me out as different from most people, but with hindsight, I can see it clearly. There are many occasions when I can remember someone staring at me, but not knowing why they were doing it or what they were expecting from me.

It's not a complete inability to read faces and body language. I can see the obvious emotions so long as I can see the entire face, but the nuance is something else. During the assessment, I found it almost impossible to determine the emotions a person was feeling just by indirectly looking at their eyes. This is important because from an autistic point of view, neurotypicals rarely say what they mean directly and expect us to either infer meaning from their words or see it in their faces. Our limited ability to read faces is a source of regular annoyance for many neurotypicals who expect that we'll know what they're thinking or feeling. In truth, we can see tight-lipped pouting, but it often makes no sense to us because we don't know why they're doing it.

Conversely, neurotypical people often make mistakes when interpreting what autistic people are thinking. We often have flat facial expressions and a flat tone of voice which can lead to misunderstandings when it's being assumed, for example, that we're scowling, frowning or not happy about something. In fact, it's just that our face isn't reflecting our emotions. This could also, in part, connect with our limited ability to read faces in others – if we can't see nuance, how can we show it? The autistic lack of facial expression can also happen when distracted by our thoughts and we're, therefore, not aware of what our faces are doing. The phrases 'cheer up, it might never happen' and 'it can't be that bad' aren't just annoying, they're patronising, too.

It's known that autistic people can struggle with making eye contact. I wonder if this contributes to why we can't read emotions around the eyes. How can we learn to recognise emotions around people's eyes when we struggle to look people in the eye? Makes sense? Problems associated with eye contact don't end here, either.

Another issue that can create confusion or misunderstanding is the belief that those who don't make eye contact are shifty or dishonest. Autistic people find direct eye contact uncomfortable. For us, it's an intense experience. For some autistic people, direct eye contact is even painful.

Smash The Boulder

Maybe where neurotypicals are concerned, the assumption of dishonesty could be true, but it's an assumption that harms autistic people. Most of us have elevated levels of integrity yet stand accused, or suspected, of being untrustworthy or hiding something just because we struggle to look others in the eye.

To this day, I look at the ground when I'm walking. I don't even realise I'm doing it because it's instinctive to me. I've also noticed that when I'm driving, I'm unconsciously registering number plates of vehicles on the other side of the road as they approach me. How can I know I'm doing this if it's unconscious? Well, every now and again, I recognise one. I'm not even one of those autists who can recite number plates, and if asked, I wouldn't be able to, but when I see one I'm familiar with, I know it. It's only having recognised the number plate that I glance up to acknowledge the driver. Otherwise, I never look directly at other drivers.

Another difference between autistic and neurotypical people that can cause problems, regards touching. Fortunately for us, this isn't as big an issue as it used to be thanks to awareness growing in the wider community about respecting other people's personal space, but it can still crop up sometimes. We aren't comfortable being touched or touching other people. We're not comfortable putting our arms around someone and often look awkward when doing things we believe are appropriate in the circumstances, but which stretch our comfort zones.

Because of this, our attempts to help someone feel better may be of a more practical nature, which often leads to the accusation of lacking empathy. Not so. Autists may show it differently, but we feel the pain more than most because of our histories. If anything, autistic people can feel empathetic towards others too much, particularly if we're sensitive to the distress of others. Worse than this can be how an autist may put their arms around someone believing it's what they're expected to do, but it's not what the other person wants at all. Autistic people often misread, or miss altogether, social cues.

Despite this, however, I worked in the community care industry for between twelve and thirteen years. Most neurotypicals couldn't do that job and will happily admit to the fact. My mother asked me how I could do it and the answer was simple: compassion. However hard you may think it would be for anyone to do what a care worker does; it's always harder for the person receiving the care. Autists don't lack empathy any more than neurotypicals do. We may need to be told what people are thinking or how they're feeling because we aren't able to read it in their face, but that's not the same thing. We can usually relate to the emotion once we know what it is, even if we don't experience it in the same way or for the same reasons. Conversely, we can sometimes struggle to recognise what we're feeling or give our feelings a name, but most of us will accept we're walking contradictions, anyway.

I think the need to empathise partly led to my interest in books. Autistic people develop intense interests in many subjects. Sometimes the interest only lasts a few weeks or months. Others can last for years. My enduring interest is books. From the moment I could read, I was never without one.

In a book, the author writes the main character's inner dialogue directly on the page. I didn't have to second guess anything, or at least, not as much. For me, stories told in writing provided a way into understanding and relating to people that I simply couldn't achieve from direct contact, or the television, alone. I also received the main character's perception of what other characters were feeling. Books enabled me to connect and empathise with other people, even if they were only fictional. I couldn't always do that with the real people around me, not because I lacked empathy, but because I couldn't read others in the same way that most people can.

The downside of reading so many books was that I was a huge fan of mysteries and thrillers. In this genre, authors always portray the detective as a flawed character, and unlike other works of fiction, the detective rarely undergoes personal growth or change. I never knew the characters were flawed by design and these flawed characters might have had too big an influence upon me for far too long! There again, my bolshy persona came in extremely useful as I was growing up. When the criticisms increased and I felt the wrath of those who believed I should know better by now, even though my brain would never develop in the same way as theirs, my hard exterior was more than body armour; it kept many potential bullies and dictators at a distance verbally, too.

Maybe my love of detective stories is the reason I like people who are unashamedly flawed. We're all flawed and I've always respected those who refuse to bend to the demands of others, but maybe the question we should ask is why some flaws are acceptable while others aren't? I haven't imagined that others always perceive my flaws as appalling, while finding the flaws of others understandable or amusing. But it's always me who's perceived as the rude or thoughtless one when I could say the same thing about them.

Eliza Jane Blake

Despite never being deliberately rude, or intending to cause offense, neurotypicals often interpret my words or manner as rude because of our different communication styles. Unfortunately, the days of me apologising for that are gone. Until I see others attempting to meet me halfway, I won't apologise anymore. Others may choose to see my choice of words as deliberately offensive, but that's their interpretation. They can just as easily choose to assume the best, rather than the worst.

This is the reason education is so important. There are so many miscommunications and misinterpretations between neurotypicals and autists that without a willingness from both sides to understand the other, we'll never bridge the gap and autistic people will continue to be side-lined and discriminated against in the workplace, regardless of the many positives that come from employing us.

I've seriously considered getting a tattoo on my arm that says 'it's not personal' because this is the biggest trial we face as autistic people. We live in a society that places a massive value on social skills when those skills are a neurotypical interpretation of what social looks like. By attempting to recognise the differences, maybe we can smooth the path to mutual acceptance and understanding because right now, the differences that exist between us on a social level, often result in autistic people being shunned in such a way that it can feel like we've been mistaken for dangerous.

The level of distrust and contempt that's levelled at us smacks of fear when we're often the most genuine people in the world. Psychopaths can be charming – think Ted Bundy. The traits that are presumed dangerous, such as the flat facial expression and voice, lack of eye contact and the avoidance

Smash The Boulder

of social connection, are autistic traits to be expected as part of our neurotype. We aren't psychopaths or dangerous, and if we were, we'd be much more accomplished at putting on a neurotypical front.

There are people who accuse us of being narcissistic, but this again, isn't true. Many autistic people can be insular, but that doesn't stop us from caring about others or feeling others' pain. Narcissists may not lack empathy in the sense that they can relate to what someone may have felt; they just don't care about it. They might even enjoy seeing the pain and feel powerful because of it, particularly if they caused it, but we don't. If anything, we feel others' pain too much. People may not realise autists have empathy, but that doesn't mean we don't have any.

Perhaps more to the point, this accusation that we lack empathy often stems from neurotypicals believing that we're too blunt and honest, and that if we had empathy for others, we'd be more considerate about how we speak to people, but this is, perhaps, the biggest misunderstanding of all. How we speak to people has nothing to do with lacking empathy; it's a consequence of our communication style. Not only that, but we can level the same accusation at them.

When neurotypicals accuse autists of lacking empathy, they're speaking from their own frame of reference, which is limited by their own experience and the erroneous belief that all human brains work in the same way and, therefore, share the same needs. Neurotypicals will accuse autists of being too direct, but from an autistic point of view, we find the neurotypical style too vague and dishonest for our communication needs. How we communicate verbally reflects an important difference in how our brains function. To understand it, we need to look at how our brains process information.

Oh Literally!

We all know communication is a complicated dance. There are so many things going on at once: the facial expression, the tone of voice, the volume of voice, the body posture, the choice of language, even the situation will affect how people communicate with each other. Besides all this, autistic people also process information differently and this adds another dimension to misunderstandings in communication between us.

Autistic people are literal thinkers. Phrases like 'pigs might fly' and 'raining cats and dogs' made no sense to me when I was a child. To this day, I still think raining cats and dogs is the most ridiculous thing I've ever heard. I'm sure there's a story to its history, but to me, it will always be nonsensical. However, neurotypical communication is littered with absurdities like this. Just as neurotypical people find the autistic style of communication offensive, we often find the 'typical' style offensive and confusing. We don't understand why people are incapable of just saying what they mean. Why the need to speak in code all the time? Why be so vague?

Clear communication, lacking in ambiguity, is crucial for autistic people. It's a massive source of frustration when neurotypicals don't say what they mean, but expect us to understand them, regardless. Because of literal interpretation, we won't process their communication in the intended way. Likewise, our communications are direct because that's how our brains process information. We'll ask a direct question to receive a direct answer.

The only thing more frustrating for us than neurotypical communication that goes around the houses, up the back alley and through the cat-flap instead of using the front door, is when we communicate unambiguously, but the neurotypical receiving the communication insists on searching for a subtext that doesn't exist. The result being a nonsensical answer to what was actually a simple and unremarkable question. I can't count the number of times neurotypical answers have confused me and I've pointed out, 'that's not what I asked you.'

The literal thinking and direct communication style of autistic people is often a source of distrust for neurotypicals. Our outright style can upset neurotypical sensibilities, but it's only a difference in style brought about by the different way in which our brains process information. We don't intend to cause offense. Our communication style isn't reflective of a lack of empathy, or care for the feelings of others, it's a consequence of how our brains work.

Smash The Boulder

Most of us can't communicate in a neurotypical way: it simply makes little sense to us. People often accuse autists of rudeness when all we did was communicate in our native autistic tongue. Unfortunately, not only do neurotypicals believe they're justified in this accusation of rudeness, but they also believe they're justified in punishing us for such a blatant breach of protocol.

Neurotypicals often believe that we need to learn and they're going to teach us! But as our communication style reflects different brain chemistry and isn't born from a desire to offend, the pushy, combative intention showed by some people, to change us into them, is at worst inappropriate and arrogant, and at best, misguided. As I've said, we find the neurotypical style every inch as offensive and thoughtless, but that's never factored in when we're being condemned by our neurotypical colleagues.

This propensity for punishing us breeds our distrust of neurotypicals and contributes to why we find it so hard to engage in communication with them – often taking active steps to avoid it where possible. The awareness that we're likely to be negatively or harshly judged is always there. It's understandable that we'd want to avoid that.

The different wiring in our brains needs recognition for what it really is, and our communication style needs to be acknowledged as no more wrong than the neurotypical communication style. Maybe the creator ran out of blue wires and used red instead! It doesn't have to be an issue. We can choose acceptance and tolerance over rigid demands of compliance.

For example, if an autist asks a neurotypical a direct question about why they've done something, they've done so because they're interested in knowing. But the neurotypical usually interprets the question as some sort of slur on their judgement. They assume that someone would only ask if they thought their reasons were wrong, but we wouldn't be questioning their judgement. We only ask because we genuinely want to understand the thought process that led to the decision.

Autists love to debate, not to annoy others, but to improve understanding and consider problems from multiple angles to aid decision making. Autists trade in facts, not assumptions, and we can't make important decisions without knowing all the facts.

But if it's not our communication style that's being misinterpreted, it's probably our sense of humour. The things we find funny rarely tally with our neurotypical colleagues, who will often find our sense of humour offensive. To them, it seems we laugh at random things or things they don't consider funny.

For example, we laugh when neurotypicals complain about something as if they're hard-done-by, when they could've easily avoided whatever consequences they're annoyed about by taking a different action. We aren't judging them for what they did, we just find the complaint amusing. Why whine about something they've brought upon themselves and could've easily avoided, but chose not to?

Neurotypicals will often assume that we're laughing at them personally, when it's the action that's amused us, rather than the person. These differences will usually tie back to our literal-thinking minds. Neurotypicals won't interpret the situation in the same way and therefore will make assumptions about why we found something funny when they aren't seeing the joke. Literal interpretation and our inherent honesty will often be at the root.

Another common reason is because the greater stimulation of autistic brains compared to neurotypical brains, combined with an enhanced ability to recognise patterns, leads to us making connections to things that don't occur to neurotypicals. These connections may seem completely abstract, but to us, our brains have jumped through a chain of connected thoughts to arrive at the obscure and seemingly irrelevant.

Conversely, we often find the neurotypical sense of humour far from funny – usually because they're laughing at how our brains work. Neurotypical training from birth tells them we're wrong because only idiots have brains that function like ours, and so they ridicule us when we misinterpret their actions and words through an autistic lens.

However, it might not be about something we've said or misinterpreted, but could just as easily relate to a sensitivity we have to which neurotypicals can't relate. Or often it'll be because someone else who's different, for whatever reason, is being mocked and ridiculed for their difference. (Yes, I'm very sensitive to that one and give very short shrift when I see it.) The analogy I used earlier, comparing us to being from the moon, is quite accurate. The gap that separates us is significant and creates problems in relating from both sides.

We don't recognise hierarchies in the same way as neurotypicals and this can also lead to misunderstandings. With everything I've already mentioned in mind, I'm going to provide an example of how all of this can play out. I've debated and argued with myself about including this and as much as I know the reaction it's going to get, I'm going to do it, because there's no point in ignoring or downplaying reality. What will follow is a classic example that shows how society rejects autistic traits, mocks those who exhibit them and treats us with contempt. Expect to roar with laughter, gasp, sneer, shake your head or scowl, because that's the accepted response in a neurotypical world. Here goes...

Once upon a time, while working in a supermarket, I was busy opening a box with my head down when a customer approached and asked me, before my brain had time to compute she was there, 'is there a tall person who could reach something?' Now, reading this, most of you will probably think this was a simple and understandable question, but from an autistic point of view, it wasn't clear enough.

Let me explain. Because I hadn't seen her approach and hadn't prepared myself for a question, the response that automatically came out of my mouth was, 'yes, I should think so!' Simultaneously, I looked up and noticing that she was considerably taller than me, said, 'it's certainly not going to be me though, is it?' (I laughed.) Strangely, she didn't seem impressed.

Now, I completely understand that you think I was being rude. I can hear the 'Oh My Gods' from here, but I wasn't being intentionally rude. The first part of my answer was an honest, immediate response to her actual question and incidentally, to an autistic person, her question was ridiculous – of course there'll be someone tall enough to reach something! Then there's the worst bit, the second thing I said.

I'm quite short and often have problems reaching items from the top shelf. When I need help in a supermarket, I seek someone who works there who's clearly tall enough to help me. Never, ever, not once, have I asked for help from a person who is smaller than I am, because that would just be silly and a waste of somebody's time, i.e., they're not tall enough to help me and I'm just as capable of glancing along a few aisles in search of someone who can, as they are. I wouldn't expect a short person to know where the tall people are or to stop what they're doing to find one for me. It's not like, 'where are the eggs?' Supermarkets don't stack the tall people on an identifiable shelf that staff can direct customers to or store them in the freezer until they're needed by the short people, and since most supermarket workers have legs, they're free to roam the store and could be anywhere. Therefore, as a customer, I would look for an appropriate person myself.

So, getting back to her question: 'is there a tall person who can reach something?' What she wanted to know, and therefore should have asked, was, 'would you mind finding someone who's tall enough to get something down for me, please?' Had she asked that question, an accurate reflection of what she wanted, my answer would have been, 'sure.' Instead, I'm branded rude and unhelpful.

Nope, I'm the most helpful person you could ever wish to meet. I read somewhere, I can't remember where, a claim that autistic people don't learn to communicate instinctively like neurotypicals do. To me, this is short-sighted nonsense that reflects majority arrogance and ignorance. In truth, neurotypicals speak neurotypical, and autists speak autistic. Our communication style is just as instinctive to us as the neurotypical style is to them. As I've already said, autistic brains process information differently than neurotypical people. That's not a choice. It's how our brains work. This is also why we experience so many misunderstandings during communication and why I, like many autistic people, will always favour written communication over verbal, every time. The lack of immediacy gives me the opportunity to consider what I'm being asked before I respond. It gives me a chance to translate the meaning of what I'm being asked. It also gives me the opportunity to consider my own words for meaning and tone. (See, I can't be that bad if I care about it.)

In that woman's eyes I was being rude, and in this world, people assume that rudeness is a choice and bad choices are things to be punished and eliminated. I wasn't rude to that woman. My brain merely responded to the actual question she asked. It isn't even the case that I was deliberately rude when I pointed out that it wouldn't be me who could help her. I didn't laugh *at* her; I laughed because she thought someone else should find a tall person on her behalf.

Unfortunately, I hadn't had time to prepare or hide my own thoughts and autists don't recognise hierarchical systems in the same way neurotypicals do. This is a classic example of how that may present itself.

Please don't make another inaccurate assumption on the back of this, though. We recognise we're required to take direction from supervisors or managers and do so willingly and politely, but while neurotypicals recognise worth and importance like a diagonal line that's elevated from where the masses inhabit the lowest point and the minority of elite people live at the top, autists see a level field. We don't recognise any person being more worthy than another and therefore don't bow to perceived self-importance.

It's well documented that autistic people speak to a cleaner in the same way they speak to a CEO. Yes, each person is being paid to do a job and the pay others may receive might be more depending on the job they do, but a higher paid job doesn't make a person superior – this is a personal judgement that suits their ego and personal criteria. In our eyes, the person who's courteously polite to the cleaner will always be a superior human to the one who behaves condescendingly to those they perceive as less than themselves.

So, the job any person does may be superior to the job I do, but each person is not their job. It's just what they do within the organisation and everybody's replaceable.

Anyway, back to the incident at the supermarket. I can well imagine this scenario being used for training as a lesson in what not to do. Indeed, I've sat through many training sessions where the trainer mocked my brain function in this way. People all over the world have used examples like this to show how not to do customer service, and every time it happens, laughter ensues, eyes roll, and comments like, 'as if we'd speak to someone like that' and 'only a moron would do that', follow.

The point is, saying you mustn't do this is too easy, but the difference in how neurotypical people communicate compared to how autistic people communicate is about brain chemistry. The neurotypical way is no more instinctive to us than the autistic way is to them. Unfortunately, knowing the difference on an intellectual level will never change this truth and it isn't right to brand the autistic style of communication as wrong and the neurotypical style as right. Both are equally valid.

Perhaps more to the point, assumptions that autistic people are stupid aren't true. Yes, we process information differently and communicate in a way neurotypicals find as annoying as we find theirs, but we're not morons! In theory, we could just as easily mock or condemn neurotypical people for not being clear in the first place and for harbouring ego-driven self-importance. 'Six of one and half a dozen of the other' – to use a neurotypical turn of phrase.

This is a classic example of how an awareness of our differences is essential if the judgements are to stop. Neurotypicals may take offense, harbour resentments and demand punishments because they find autists offensive, but it shouldn't be all about them and their needs. Understanding is the only way for us all to lead more peaceful and relaxed lives. This must be a better option than believing, or choosing to assume, that others want to cause offense.

Another example happened at my son's school. I can't remember the occasion that dragged us parents into the school hall to receive a talk from the headteacher but there we all were, and he started speaking, and naturally, a mobile phone beeped.

Everybody laughed because there's always one, right? But then everyone noticed the headteacher scowling towards the offending beep and suddenly, the hall fell silent as the parents lowered their heads in shame. Naturally, I laughed even louder. It was so ridiculous. I couldn't believe all these grown adults who'd left school many years before, being intimidated by a headteacher who clearly lacked a sense of humour. That he didn't seem to realise his school hall was full of parents rather than children was bad enough, but that they all reacted like naughty children caught with their fingers in the cookie jar was just too hilarious for me. My laughing embarrassed my son, although I'm very pleased to say that he now also thinks it was funny.

Of course, neurotypicals would probably attribute my laughter to a lack of impulse control and say that they also thought it was funny, but the headteacher is high enough to be acknowledged as an authority and afforded the courtesy he believes he deserves. Maybe my laughter was more about impulse control, but then, I don't recognise hierarchical structures like neurotypicals do, so why would I need to control the impulse to laugh?

I'm sure I'm not the only autist who would've found that man's arrogance and warped sense of self-importance, in the presence of such lowly parents, funny. However, lacking impulse control is another common accusation that's thrown at autists and while it may be true in some respects, this observation about our character developed by comparison to neurotypical standards, too. Neurotypicals judge everything we say, do and think against their own standards as if there's a right and a wrong way, rather than just a difference based on brain function.

As blunt or direct as neurotypicals perceive us, consider this: autists communicate in the style they need to receive. Read that again. Not only do we not recognise hierarchies like neurotypicals do, but we also need clarity and certainty in all verbal communication, otherwise our literal brains misread the intention or drown in confusion.

Hints rarely register. We often struggle with verbal instructions, not only when they lack clarity but also when given too many upfront. Neurotypicals rarely say what they mean, expecting others to infer meaning, but we struggle with that.

To avoid misunderstandings, be direct. Avoid subtext. Make no assumptions. Dare I say, see how difficult it is to communicate the autistic way when it's not your instinctive language or communication style? If you're neurotypical, see how hard it is to interpret everything you hear literally when this isn't your default setting. Note the intensity of concentration needed to maintain it and how often it breaks. But our differences in brain function don't end here. We differ in how we approach problem solving, too.

Bottoms-Up

So, we know autistic people process information differently. This is clear in both verbal and non-verbal communication, but it also affects how autists make their decisions and seek solutions to problems.

Top-down thinking is a known characteristic of neurotypical people. Autistic people, however, are bottom-up thinkers. We approach problem solving in diametrically opposite ways.

While autists make their decisions based on facts, neurotypicals make their decisions based on assumptions that factor in past performance. There are pros and cons in both methods, but this is a crucial difference in how our brains function and one that needs to be understood.

We ask a lot of questions. In fact, autistic people have a tremendous capacity for annoying neurotypical people purely by asking these questions. Not only do we need clarity in communication, but we also need to know details before we can make our decisions. We need to know all the relevant facts.

So, the difference in the 'facts versus assumptions' approach affects our understanding of each other's brain function in several ways.

When making decisions, autists are thorough in ascertaining the facts so we can avoid mistakes. This means that the process can take time; usually more time than neurotypicals welcome. However, our solutions are usually complete, well thought out and good for the long-term. Unfortunately, neurotypicals seem to hate us for it.

Neurotypical people make their decisions based on past performance and this involves making assumptions – sometimes a lot of them. As a method, it can be a bit hit and miss and may not get to the root of a problem, but the prevailing opinion is often that sticking-plaster solutions are good enough. Everybody wants a fast answer so they can move on and the neurotypical method of making decisions achieves this. From their point of view, not only do autists ask too many questions, but we're also guilty of over-thinking problems.

From an autist's point of view, neurotypicals make an incredible number of assumptions without checking they're on the right track. We find this tendency to make assumptions every inch as annoying as they find our need to ask questions. Not taking the care to do something right, and get it right the first time, frustrates autistic people and this doesn't just apply to deciding how to solve a particular problem, it can play out in other ways, too.

Smash The Boulder

Let me give you an example that shows this 'fact versus assumption' method of processing information. It borders on the ridiculous, but it conveys the point.

Some years ago, I was working in an office and suddenly heard screaming coming from the next room, so I went to investigate. Well, you would, wouldn't you? Was there a fire? Had the roof caved in? Had someone solved the 'who came first, chicken or egg problem', then fallen off their chair, banged their head and broken an arm? Not quite. I found three colleagues, all women, kneeling on top of desks and screeching for no apparent reason. They pointed at a bag on another desk shouting, 'there's a mouse in the bag!'

I honestly don't understand why a mouse is reason enough to kneel on a desk and squeal, but as nobody else was going to check the bag, I did. Did I find a mouse? No, of course I didn't. I found a child's plastic toy that wasn't even a pretend mouse; it was a dinosaur. They'd reacted to an assumption without checking it for accuracy.

Here's another example to consider. About twenty years ago, I was studying accounts and exam season came around. We students were told unequivocally that experts had checked the exam papers, double checked and triple checked them, and there was absolutely no way there would ever be an error on a paper.

Fast forward to a tax exam. There were two ways of calculating an answer to the question I was looking at and, because I didn't like to assume I'd calculated it right the first time, I double-checked my original answer by using the alternative method. You've guessed it, they didn't tally. I double-checked both of my answers and arrived at the same result each time. Feeling confused and flustered, I looked around, but nobody else seemed to have any problems or concerns.

Being autistic, my stress levels escalated quickly. There couldn't be an error on the paper. We'd been told it wasn't possible. Was I doing something wrong? Why was nobody else looking confused? If there was an error on the paper, they'd tell us the error was there, right? Nobody said a word. I was tense and stressed for the rest of the exam because of this simple anomaly.

At the end of the exam, I sought the lecturer and asked if she was aware of there being an error on the paper. Dismissively, she said, 'Oh, yeah, we know.' I asked her why they hadn't mentioned it to us, and she shrugged like it wasn't important and said, 'We didn't think anybody would notice it.'

I just looked at her. Exams are stressful anyway and something like that can send an autistic person into a meltdown. She wasn't concerned, however, or apologetic that they'd known but not said anything. My distress was unimportant. She was right that nobody else had noticed it, though. Nobody else had bothered double-checking their answers. They'd just assumed they'd done it right the first time.

Another point to be aware of about making assumptions, and this is extremely important for autistic people, is that when people state something they believe to be true to an autistic person, to gauge a reaction by which they can assess the validity of their assumption, silence is not acquiescence.

Neurotypical people will always jump to the conclusion that it is, because if it wasn't, a denial would've been forthcoming, right? Wrong. This connects to literal interpretation. A statement is a statement. A question is a question. Even though I know people do this, I'll still miss it. If the penny drops at all, it won't happen until a later moment because my lack of response is instinctive. Without a question being asked, no response is appropriate.

I mentioned earlier that autists often miss hints. In this context, the statement is a hint and not only is this not compatible with the autistic way of interpreting words literally, but it also creates problems because of processing delays.

The fact we may know neurotypicals communicate like this won't over-ride the instinctive literal interpretation, and processing delays will see that we don't recognise the statement for what it is until much later, if at all.

Neurotypicals assume they've given us an opportunity to correct their assumption, but they haven't. Please, always ask what you want to know in a specific and direct manner to avoid confusion and misunderstandings.

This also applies to requests. I saw something on the internet where an autistic girl had got into an argument because her mother insisted she'd asked her to put the washing out and the autistic girl was just as adamant she hadn't. What the mother had said to her was, 'It's a lovely day, isn't it?' To which her daughter had agreed and got on with her day.

It later transpired she was supposed to have inferred from her mother's statement that she wanted her to hang the washing outside. Please know, this sort of neurotypical communication won't elicit the response hoped for from an autistic person and the upshot will be disappointment, annoyance, or resentment.

Eliza Jane Blake

A statement is a statement and a request is a request. When neurotypicals expect us to infer meaning by cloaking requests and questions as statements, we're not being rude when we ignore them because we haven't, we simply didn't receive a clear enough communication, and autists always need clarity.

Some people assume a lack of intelligence because of this, but our differences in communication style and information processing are merely a feature of our neurotype and to be expected.

There's just one more thing I'd like to draw attention to about making assumptions. Neurotypicals often gossip about and bully autistic people because of assumptions they've made about us on a personal level. Many seem to believe that gossip is harmless. This is because they want to indulge in it and it suits their purposes to believe that it's not only harmless, but normal human behaviour and therefore perfectly acceptable. But when their gossip involves speculating and making assumptions about a person who's autistic, a person they don't understand, it's not much of a stretch to recognise why this can be so harmful.

Please consider the implications of making assumptions about a person whose brain functions differently. How reliable are those assumptions likely to be? Neurotypicals relentlessly hold autists to neurotypical standards when those standards aren't compatible with our wiring. We often face accusations of misdemeanours we don't recognise, simply because a neurotypical has made an inaccurate assumption.

The neurotypical omission to check the validity of their assumptions, or at best, to only consider them against their own standards – which are based on experiences that most likely involve other neurotypicals – is possibly one of the most damaging things autists live with.

So, we look the same as neurotypicals but are inherently different, but how can neurotypicals recognise autistic people and spare us the indignity of uncomfortable and unfair speculation? Is this even possible? Yes, it is, even though looks can be deceiving.

Looks Deceive

For some neurodivergent people, for example, those with Downs Syndrome, there's a visual element to their condition that's readily recognisable. This isn't the case with autistic people, although I've read that wide foreheads and widely spaced eyes can be common. I don't have either, but my eyes can seem to stare as can most other autists when we're not concentrating on how our face might look to others – which, in my case, is most of the time!

Some autists have an ungainly gait because having an autistic brain has the potential to affect both major and minor motor function. My major motor function is fine, but I've always had untidy and inconsistent handwriting because of minor motor function issues. At school, my teachers consistently downgraded me in English class because of it. Reliably, there are only two ways to know what an autist looks like. The first is if they tell you they're autistic, the other is by recognising traits.

Sounds simple, but naturally, it's not quite that straightforward. There's a common saying within the autistic community that if you've met one autistic person, you've met one autistic person. So, how can it be done? I mentioned before how the spectrum works. We share core characteristics and it's only the degree to which any of those traits affect an autist that creates the differences between us, hence the saying mentioned. There will also be differences resulting from personality, various levels of intelligence and the consequence of life experience, but these factors aren't traits that separate autistic people from neurotypical people. They're just a reflection of being human.

The core traits are differences in communication, social interaction, and restricted and repetitive behaviours. Officially, at its most basic, that's it. How these three core traits present is far more complex, though. We've already looked at communication styles and social interaction differences and an observation based on these differences will provide many clues, but there are other indicators it can help to be aware of.

People often accuse autistic people of being childlike, and there are several reasons for this. Some of us can relate to the accusation, while others don't recognise themselves as childlike at all. Like neurotypicals, we're individuals.

For me, my childlike self is energetic, inquisitive, happy-go-lucky and a much nicer person to be around than my masked or protective self, who, to put it bluntly, is downright miserable most of the time. However, when I'm true to myself, I'm subjected to so many assumptions of intellectual impairment, or harsh judgements and criticism for not acting my age, I find the pressure relentless. When I mask up, I'm also harshly judged and criticised because I get it wrong.

It takes a massive amount of energy to pretend to be somebody I'm not every time I walk out of my front door. Some autists may sustain it; I never could. I would go to work, immerse myself in whatever I was working on, lose awareness of my surroundings, and people would accuse me of ignoring them, being rude, deliberately causing offense, or simply not trying to fit in.

I refute all these allegations. Ignoring people who've done me no harm isn't what I do. I do, however, slip into hyper-focus when I'm enjoying my work. This is common to autists and other neurodivergent people. When we're interested in what we're doing, we can drop into a state of concentration so intense that everything else fades into non-existence. Once, someone spoke to me in a room that was otherwise silent, but I didn't hear them. It's easy to see how someone could interpret that as being ignored.

Anyway, I digress. It's true, we can be unaware of how we come across, particularly when distracted or concentrating on a task. We may still like cartoons and cuddly toys, but so what? I still like to sit on the floor. Others like to walk barefoot to feel the surface. I feel like I'm being forced to wear a mask when I'm compelled to comply with neurotypical expectations or when I'm being belittled for being my true self. I can also sound like a child when I talk – usually if I'm tired or not concentrating on how I'm coming across, and this is also quite common with autistic people. We can appear more childlike when we're unmasked because we're being our true selves.

Smash The Boulder

Incidentally, the way I digressed from talking about childlike personas into talking about hyper-focus and back again, is another sign to be aware of. The autistic brain never stops. The internal dialogue we experience is a constant stream and well known for jumping from topic to topic in a way that can often seem quite random to other people. It happens because our brains make connections that aren't always obvious to those around us. Autistic people often have enhanced pattern recognition skills, which, when combined with a brain that's always running a marathon, can take others by surprise with the speed of our apparently random gear changes.

So, are autistic people childlike? Yes, we can be. Are we childish? No. This is an assumption born from a construct created by neurotypicals to determine what is childish behaviour and what is adult behaviour. It's based upon neurotypical development, processing, and expectations. For us, our inquisitive minds keep us young. So long as we're breathing, we'll be interested in how and why things work.

So, autistic people often have a young energy, and this shows when we're our authentic selves. We like what we like and we'd like to enjoy our interests without judgement, condemnation, or ridicule, just like neurotypicals do. Some of us like games, cuddly toys, child fantasy books, Lego, kites, computers, trains, whatever. Basically, the things we enjoyed as children may persist into adulthood, or at least they would if we could be ourselves, without being mocked or reined in by those who find our interests embarrassing or inconvenient. We may well express childlike delight in things, but so what? The point is, it's not society's right to dictate what others should enjoy, or what other people should do with their time.

Eliza Jane Blake

This constant picking at who we are and what we like may be born from the neurotypical need for social connection. People who don't comply with the unwritten rules and expectations of the neurotypical society have their acceptance withdrawn until they do. To neurotypicals, being socially abandoned is the worst fate that can befall them. So, fitting in with others is a much higher priority for neurotypicals than for autists. Neurotypicals believe they're helping us by constantly discouraging those aspects about us they consider undesirable or inappropriate.

Autists want acceptance too, but not by fitting in with neurotypical expectations. We are who we are and we're happy with who we are; or at least we would be if not for the constant criticism and fault-finding. But for neurotypicals, this need to fit in is so intense, and the corresponding fear of the consequences of breaking those unwritten rules, so severe, they're quick to point out when autists are getting it wrong. And when they're not trying to help us, they're trying to change us. There's a positive angle to the intrusion, but unfortunately, there's also a negative one. Manipulative people want to influence us. Control us. Often, they make a beeline for us because they think we're an easy target.

The thing is, though, while autistic people also need social connection, we don't need it to the degree that neurotypical people do and so this, combined with our very different brain wiring, means their efforts to punish us in this way don't always have the desired effect. Don't misunderstand me, it hurts and we don't like being mistreated. We don't understand the capacity for spite and nastiness shown by some neurotypicals. But it won't change us and that's what the punishment brigade can't understand.

Smash The Boulder

If you want to know how to recognise an autistic person, look to the outer edge of social or workplace groups. Often that's where we'll be; either because we're being punished, or because we're trying to stay out of the way to avoid it. It's a horrible truth, but the reality of our existence in the neurotypical world is often one of exile, whether it's a consequence of rejection by the pack, or our own choice to distance ourselves from hostility, judgement and misunderstandings.

Of course, if we want to, while neurotypicals are sneering, scowling or avoiding us, we can bite back. Some of us learn to do it loudly and ferociously. Autistic people can argue that the neurotypical need to fit in and follow the crowd to ensure the continuation and security of their social connections is their own self-imposed prison. A restriction they choose to accept born from a need to be accepted, or a desire to lead the pack, but that's only our perception of neurotypical behaviour because our needs aren't the same. In modern society, however, none of us should expect everyone to play the same game. Difference is normal.

Younger autistic people often want the approval of the pack and may be prepared to compromise to achieve it, but older autists are more likely to have tired of the game and, when we take a step back to distance ourselves from the chaos, that's what it looks like to us: a game. Some sort of tedious party dance. Neurotypicals have subjected me to this punishment charade, so many times, I won't deny that my reaction now is to roll my eyes and blank those who like to indulge in it.

Ultimately, we won't make the same effort as neurotypicals to be part of the pack. Often because we don't think our rejection is fair or justified to start with. Then there's an element of not needing to be around others to the same extent, and while acceptance is preferable to being shunned, not if the price is changing our entire being to satisfy the demands of others.

We simply don't recognise hierarchies like neurotypical people do. It's not for me to burst anyone's bubble, but while overly demanding neurotypicals may think we should consider their acceptance and attention the most valuable thing on Earth, we'll soon find something else to do if it's not forthcoming. Or maybe it's just that society has shunted us to the fringes for so long that we've grown comfortable with it, or at the least, have accepted it as our peaceful place. Society should accept autistic people just like every other minority group, but acceptance, like love, isn't real if it's conditional.

The concept of diversity has been around for a while now, and I hope the day comes when it doesn't have to be a hot topic. It's important we avoid limiting respect to some groups at the expense of others. Ignorance has much to answer for, but as the saying goes, ignorance isn't a defence. Why should people have to be a total reflection of the pack before the pack will find it in their heart to treat them with basic courtesy? Is this not a reflection of insecurity and a need to maintain control?

Minorities aren't a different tribe and don't represent a threat to the majority. Both local and wider communities follow the same laws and usually share the same or similar values. While the tribe has grown drastically in the numbers that make up communities, the closed mentality to difference passed down through the generations by our ancestors has changed little. At least, not unless forced to by the threat of intense shaming if people don't comply. How can any society claim to be advocates for inclusivity if they don't recognise humans as one tribe?

Being able to understand myself, and be myself, for the first time, has been difficult, but also a revelation. I hadn't realised how stressed and on-edge I was all the time until I received my diagnosis and dared to embrace who I really am as opposed to who those around me demand I be. Whether we're like everybody else, or completely different, we're still human.

It's common for autistic people to be considered either too much or too little. This is also a consequence of our brain function, but it's not the intention of autists to make others feel uncomfortable and because of our limited ability to read non-verbal cues (faces and body language) many of us don't realise when we're doing this. It could relate to the things we talk about, how we say them, not taking neurotypical hints to stop talking, or being too friendly or not friendly enough. I mentioned before about the way neurotypicals communicate being instinctive to them, but not to us. Our confusion is another sign that can identify us.

But knowing this doesn't change anything because autistic people also have an instinctive way of communicating – a way that neurotypicals have tried to eradicate because they don't like it – but humans speak many languages and it often seems to me that this is our real problem. The only way to iron out the misunderstandings is if we're all educated to recognise these differences and accept them for what they are rather than fight against them.

The medical community acknowledges ASD as a neurodevelopmental disorder and it's this aspect of our brain

Eliza Jane Blake

function that often leads neurotypicals to assume we're stuck in an age-related way, but we grow too.

We Grow Too

Most information written about the autistic neurotype focuses on children and many people believe it's a recent phenomenon rather than a recent awareness of a long-standing difference. As I've mentioned before, most people don't recognise autistic traits unless they have an autistic family member, usually a child, or they're a trained professional.

By comparison to children, information about autistic adults is scant at best, but autistic children don't grow out of their autistic brains and autistic adults haven't acquired them. Some people peddle the idea that a child can become less autistic with therapy, but as our difference is a consequence of biology, that can't happen. This misconception comes about because some autists learn to mask their authentic selves, but that's not the same thing.

Eliza Jane Blake

An autistic person will, however, grow and mature, just as neurotypicals do. Even if we come across as childlike, our intelligence and maturity still progress, but because doctors recognise having an autistic brain as having a 'neurodevelopmental disorder', this can create confusion.

I object to the label of a disorder, but what they're recognising is that our brains develop inconsistently when compared to neurotypical brains. Contrary to what many people believe, most autistic people don't have learning disabilities, nor is our intelligence or maturity stunted, even if progress is slower.

A childlike persona could contribute to the erroneous belief that autistic people have a limited mental age and the most probable cause of this misinterpretation is likely to stem not so much from our speech, interests or tastes, but from our communication style.

The combination of literal interpretation and direct honesty is associated with children. It's this that neurotypicals expect adults to have grown out of. But we never do. Some may learn to hide it behind a mask, but our default setting doesn't change. Society often accuses adults who still think and communicate in this way of lacking a filter and many assume intellectual disability or deficit because of it. In truth, the expectation is entirely based upon neurotypical progression.

Neurotypicals try hard to force our communication and information processing style out of us, and it's in combination with the lack of expected neurotypical social skills that most will not only assume stunted intellectual development, but also rudeness.

Smash The Boulder

My family denied the existence of difference and didn't tolerate the non-compliance of expected standards. My older relatives passed down the intense brainwashing their own relatives had drilled into them about what an acceptable person looks like and left me in no doubt that I fell short. The way I communicated caused the biggest annoyance and frustration, and I'm not alone in experiencing this. It's quite common for autistic people to lack confidence and self-esteem because of all the judgements people make about us, not just the wider community, but often by our own families, too.

My family expected me to settle into a relationship, use my brain to forge a suitable career, buy a house and have children. They expected their priorities to be mine and my failures (in their eyes) only added to the many ways I disappointed or frustrated them. Their priorities were, of course, adopted because society had taught them that they mattered. On another level, society and acquaintances shamelessly drilled into me that popularity and having lots of friends was essential to being worthy as a person, with obvious implications when I didn't. But this nonsense is a neurotypical construct that reflects neurotypical values and aspirations, too. It doesn't recognise that others have different priorities and that those priorities aren't wrong.

How often do we see a grieving person on television saying how the deceased was popular and loved by everyone? It's like popularity is a holy grail; the definition of a decent person living a successful and worthy life. It's also a standard that many autistic people can't meet and which puts us at an automatic disadvantage in life. It causes significant harm to our self-esteem and diminishes our own priorities.

Eliza Jane Blake

As a young adult, I tried the relationship game but found the things that mattered to me never mattered at all. My wants and needs didn't matter because they were wrong or irrelevant. The message I consistently received was, therefore, that I didn't matter. A similar pattern played out where friends were concerned. I had friends in the past, but never many. In truth, this was partly to do with my limited ability to maintain friendships because social demands exceed my limits, but also because I was never the person others wanted or expected me to be.

Where both relationships and friendships are concerned, it's always my experience that people want more from me than I can give and while I will compromise, others won't. I, like many autistic people, can only juggle so many demands on my time and, in truth, I enjoy spending time on my own. I don't want to be on my own all the time, but I can't be around other people all the time, either. This is common to autistic people, but it isn't the anti-social behaviour neurotypicals assume it to be. We aren't against being social, we just aren't able to spend as much time around other people, without then needing recovery time.

I haven't done relationships or close friendships for a long time now, only acquaintances. My life is certainly less fraught and free from guilt for living this way. In my experience, when people don't get what they want, or believe they have a right to demand or expect, they become nasty and spiteful. They believe they have a right to punish me and do so. This is a pattern that I've found repeated many times. It also reflects how unwilling many people are to compromise.

And this is another common accusation that's levelled at autistic people: that we're inflexible. For context, this probably relates to our need for routine, certainty, and sameness. However, when we hear this accusation, we can't help but wonder if the neurotypicals who make that claim have looked in the mirror lately. We often see a dogged refusal to allow us to pass, or to even consider our feelings, while the neurotypical majority insist we respect their feelings.

Whatever efforts we make are never enough. So, is it the autistic community that's stunted and inflexible, or is it the neurotypical ego-centred belief that they should always receive what they want and need, and that those needs are universal, that would benefit from a re-think? For me, not being in a relationship and not having lots of friends has certainly affected my self-esteem, but only because society drilled into me it should.

So, I walked away. I stopped accepting the demands placed upon me by others that only served them at my expense. People have been too quick to assume that I've let them down or been a terrible friend/relative/colleague (delete as required) or worse, that I should be grateful to them for being prepared to be my friend when nobody else would. Walking away from it has been truly liberating.

This plays out in work situations, too. In theory, work relationships are professional, but because of the time colleagues spend together, they become more personal. As a female, I avoid connecting with female colleagues because they're more likely to pry on a personal level, judge, and reject or misinterpret my nature. Men are more likely to maintain boundaries on a personal level and are therefore easier to be around. I'm more on edge around women and constantly feel judged by them.

Eliza Jane Blake

Naturally, people misjudge this situation and gossip about it. People judge others by their own standards and neurotypicals make a lot of assumptions. I don't know if male autists have found female neurotypicals easier to be around in the workplace for the same reason or if men are just easier to be around. But in my experience, women always cause me the most problems.

As autists, we know we're different and that our priorities differ from those of neurotypical people. We know those differences generate curiosity, but we're neither exhibits in a zoo nor the curiosity act at the circus. Some consideration would go a long way.

Autists go to work, to do the work. Neurotypicals prioritise relationships with their colleagues over that. While neurotypicals will stay in a job they don't particularly enjoy if they have good relationships with their colleagues, autists will leave a job if they aren't enjoying the work. Our colleagues often reject us anyway, so it's unlikely we'd stay because of other people, unless we come across a friendly crowd that makes us welcome. We may, however, leave if the atmosphere and hostility become too intense. Often, how badly our colleagues treat us is directly proportionate to how many there are buoying each other up. People often use the pack mentality to bully us.

The nastiness and bitchiness, the intrusion into our personal lives and the punishments colleagues mete out because we're not being the person they expect us to be, may be unrelenting, but might not lead to us leaving. Instead, we may choose to keep our heads down and avoid our colleagues wherever possible. This isn't a pleasant situation to be in. Indeed, it's one for which we can expect further punishment because we're not getting along with our colleagues when companies place a disproportionately high value on this – including those who claim to be champions for diversity and inclusion. Management never seems to recognise that the intolerance and criticism the majority throw at the misunderstood minority is a pretty big hindrance to getting along, and that the ones who're different aren't solely to blame for misunderstandings.

Another consequence of avoidance is that people perceive the distance we create as a personal rejection. This isn't our intention and self-protection from hostility isn't our only motivation for doing it. I've already mentioned that autistic people can only manage a limited amount of time around other people. It's not necessarily the physical presence, although I'm not alone in finding crowds overwhelming, it's the verbal interaction.

Our struggles with small talk make us come across as awkward. We find inane chitchat not only tedious, but difficult. It's not something we can readily connect to, but people expect it from us and interpret any attempt to avoid it as a personal rejection. But it's not about them. Our discomfort and reluctance are a consequence of being out of our comfort zone.

Our preference for discussing work-related matters rather than personal, and our need to decompress after communicating with others, is a reality of our brain function, not a personal affront. It makes sense for us to limit the contact we have with others to preserve our energy levels.

Prioritising self-preservation and well-being isn't about the rejection of others and there's a lot to be gained for us by taking the time to step back and do our own thing. The sooner and more often we can do this, the healthier and happier we are.

There's been much talk in the media since the covid pandemic about the consequences of lockdown on people's mental health. The autistic community has commented online how much better we fared during this time and it's true, but only to a point. We are undeniably better at solitude than most neurotypicals, partly because we need more time to ourselves, but also because society forces isolation upon us, but we need human contact and interaction too, even if we do it differently and don't need as much. Total isolation can be just as harmful for us as it is for neurotypicals, so there was also an element of 'welcome to our world' during this time.

For me, semi-isolation is a choice now, but only because it hasn't been possible to find a workable compromise with people who believe that I'm not available enough to meet their needs. It's my experience that people are unwilling to compromise. Neurotypicals expect us to meet their standards and believe that anyone who doesn't lacks commitment or isn't interested. I can see where this belief stems from, but in relationships, for example, autists rarely stray far so long as someone isn't trying to control or dictate to them. Clingy people aren't for autists, either at home or at work. Many autistic people feel this way and most of us can relate to being on the receiving end of bullying or ridiculing in the workplace because of our lack of social connections.

Not that it's this that does the most harm. We can expect to be gossiped about and judged for not seeming to have a life according to the neurotypical construct of what that means, but our lack of social connections will usually only bring us ridicule or make us the butt of the joke. The things that get us into trouble at work are usually our communication style or struggles to control our emotions.

Management relate to how our actions or words must have offended someone and will take their side, secure that the organisation's policies frown on our way of being and will consider us to be in the wrong – often a consequence of inaccurate assumptions made by neurotypicals to explain our manner or behaviour resulting in the conclusion of us having an attitude problem. Ironically, it's the autists with learning difficulties and the most acute sensory issues that society tolerates most readily.

People find it easier when they can clearly see that someone has a disability. The problem for most autists is that we look just like everybody else. There's no flashing light on our heads to inform everyone of a different neurotype, and neurotypical people expect that anyone who's intelligent should be capable of following their unwritten social rules and conventions. To deviate from this is to show rudeness, poor character, or an undesirable personality. All three being worthy of punishment.

Autistic people, especially those without a diagnosis, often find themselves on the receiving end of plots to oust them because they don't fit in. There are a few reasons for this. The perception of being anti-social or socially awkward is one of them. A poor attitude is another, but this often stems from defensiveness brought about by too many expectations, judgements and accusations to which we don't relate.

Without a diagnosis to explain or justify the differences, management will start a file where they collect evidence to justify the sacking of their 'problem' employee, and other employees who don't like us will be quick to run to management with tales of how terrible or anti-social we are.

This has never been okay. Essentially, autistic people – regardless of whether they know it – are being dismissed from jobs in which they perform well, purely because they're not neurotypical.

It's a practice that's on a par with sacking someone for being black, gay, or of a different religion. Not liking someone isn't a reason to oust anyone from their job, but this is common in a world that doesn't want to compromise and that doesn't recognise different neurotypes.

Being autistic and therefore communicating in a way that neurotypicals perceive to be wrong, isn't a reflection of someone who hasn't grown up yet, or of someone who's too lazy to make the effort, or worse, someone who's selfish and inconsiderate of others. The most selfish, disingenuous, self-serving people I've ever met have been the most socially adept.

Unfortunately, they're also faking their desirable personality. I can't be the only one to watch them manipulate anyone they perceive as useful to them. They'll say the right thing, in the right way, to the right person at the right time and smirk as their prey falls at their feet for the price of an ego rub.

Their duplicitous nature and the inability of most in the room to realise or object to what they're doing rankles when genuine autists who care about their fellow humans continue being rejected in favour of the disingenuous.

This underhand behaviour is rarely, if ever, seen in autistic people. It's not in our make-up to want to behave in this way, although we may retaliate if mistreated. But if we call out those manipulative people who shamelessly lie about our intentions to management because they want us to be punished, they will just accuse us of lying or misunderstanding their innocent intentions. Manipulative people are such outstanding actors, they'll recite a savage sob-story and have everybody believing in their innocence in no time.

The closest autistic people come to being disingenuous is when we mask our true selves to appear as neurotypical as possible. How ironic that, in our case, the intention to deceive is a required behaviour if we're to survive in a neurotypical world.

Those autists diagnosed as children are often taught how to come across as neurotypical and those without a diagnosis may learn from neurotypical family members and others by observing those around them. This isn't, however, an easy feat and requires a plentiful supply of mental energy that will deplete throughout the course of their life.

Please know that masking isn't the simple or ideal solution to surmounting our differences and is ultimately harmful to us. It takes a massive effort to pretend to be someone that we're not every day and there comes a point (usually once an autist gets past forty) when the construct collapses. Even those who found masking relatively easy when they were young can develop problems maintaining the façade and many autistic people aren't proficient at the pretence, anyway. Worse than that, the long-term impact of masking is mental burnout and this can be physically debilitating, too.

For my part, I was never great at masking to fit in. I was successful at masking in limited ways, but I couldn't maintain the pretence for long enough to be consistent. So, most of my masking was about protection. Despite being gentle and kind by nature, I mastered aggression (not violence) like no other and it's very easy to criticise that, but when a person faces daily attacks for perceived slights and for not coming across as others believe they have a right to expect, aggression is the fastest and most efficient way of convincing someone to leave you alone.

That was the purpose of it and I know other autists have done it for the same reason. It wasn't about wanting to scare people or dictate, and it certainly wasn't about bullying, it was about needing peace and just wanting the world to get off my back and leave me alone. I don't mean others harm, but I've certainly been on the receiving end of spite and malicious behaviours by those who wish to harm me.

Autistic people can, and often do, learn over time about the differences between how our brains think compared to others. We have no choice, but the different wiring in our brains means that we only learn it on an intellectual level. The neurotypical way never becomes instinctive like it is for neurotypical people. For us, it's a process of slowly becoming aware (after a relentless barrage of accusations that we don't recognise) that other people speak a different language, but no matter how hard we try to learn and master it, it's only ever a second language and not one that we become completely proficient in or comfortable with.

Misunderstandings will always exist. Processing delays will often create delays in translation. The non-verbal elements may well pass us by. Our instinctive communication style will always lean towards literal interpretation and our responses will reflect this.

We learn and grow, just like everybody else, but we need neurotypicals to be just as aware of how to interpret our language, as they expect us to understand theirs. Then, when misunderstandings arise, both can recognise how it happened and choose the option to step back, rather than reacting to perceived slights that were never intended.

As I mentioned before, autistic brains are most easily recognised by our social differences. For us to work together in harmony, the belief in a connection between social skills and intelligence needs reconsideration. Society ties them together in the neurotypical world, in a way that doesn't apply to autistic people and does us a great injustice.

In the neurotypical world, an intelligent person will use their social skills to further their own aims and objectives. This is an intelligent thing to do, but leads to the assumption that anyone who's intelligent should also have excellent social skills.

Autistic people often struggle and face punishment, simply because people think we're smart enough to know better. Obviously, we must be choosing to be rude instead. To overcome this tangible difference in how we communicate, intelligence and social skills are best thought of as separate circuits.

By recognising ASD as a social difference, rather than believing it to be a behavioural issue, the wider world can change their perspective from one of rejection to acceptance. Assuming our differences are a behavioural issue implies a choice that autists don't have. Society needs to recognise when different brain chemistry is at play, rather than assuming rudeness and an attitude problem to be eradicated.

Differences with social interaction and communication are a fundamental part of autistic wiring and the extent of an autist's knowledge of neurotypical communication will depend upon how much support they've received in their life.

But it's the differences in how we process information and communicate that are the main issues that divide us. An intelligent autistic employee will never be an expert schmoozer, but do they really deserve to be condemned or side-lined in the workplace for that?

Autistic people are often under-employed; doing work that doesn't reflect their abilities, and that's assuming they can hold down a job at all. While society thinks itself reasonable in rejecting us, autistic people are being punished when their perceived sins are actually the traits of a recognised disability.

Only acceptance of the correct position can stop this persecution in the workplace and society's refusal to tolerate what they don't understand must change. Without doing this, we can't hope to move forward. Many autistic people are intelligent and capable of working to a high standard. It isn't true we've failed to mature, chosen to be rude, or lack empathy and consideration. Not only that, but perceived attitude problems would likely disappear if we could relax in a tolerant atmosphere instead of having to defend ourselves, or constantly be in a hypervigilant, prepared state of readiness, to defend.

But it's not only about communication style. Another element that leads to us being accused of having an attitude problem, or behavioural issues, is what neurotypicals consider reactions that aren't justified. Autistic sensory receptors typically magnify our experience of the world around us. Various stimuli, that have no effect on neurotypicals, often affect autistic people in ways they can't understand. But the

Smash The Boulder

consequences for us can be very real and, at times, overwhelming. This is another bridge we need to cross.

Can You Sense It?

Some in the neurotypical community believe that a world dominated by autistic people would be loud, overly emotional or devoid of emotion, maybe even unhinged and, of course, anti-social. I'd like to turn that on its head.

Most autistic people would accept an accusation of being contradictory. We can be the quietest and the noisiest. We can be the calmest and the most agitated. We can find quiet noises too much and loud rock music relaxing. I could go on.

We often wish we could make sense of such contradictions, but we can't. All we can do is accept what is, and when the world is too loud for us to cope with, we know the importance of finding a calm space. The upshot of not distancing ourselves when our senses become overwhelmed is traumatic, to say the least.

Smash The Boulder

Unfortunately, this socially oriented world doesn't react kindly to those who pull back from others and we know that stepping back is the best way to achieve a sense of calm when the world becomes too much. In many jobs, supervisors frown upon workers leaving the room or their desk outside of designated breaks, meaning that we have to stay where we are regardless of what may be overwhelming us.

But considering how contradictory we are, how do we know what might be a trigger? Trial and error is the answer to that and we never stop learning because triggers can change over a lifetime, but we need people to understand that when we pull back, they should let us go.

It's also worth mentioning that pulling back may not involve physically removing ourselves from the room; it could be a retreat from verbal interaction, instead. But whether physical or verbal, the worst thing anyone can do is chase after us, obstruct us from taking time out, or try to engage us in conversation. We need neurotypicals to recognise that what works for them doesn't work for us, especially when they assume we should talk about it.

Neurotypicals need to talk when they're upset, but autists often can't talk at the time and neurotypicals will misinterpret this as another personal rejection or even as sulking on our part. Often, they'll assume they've given us an opportunity to speak, but we've chosen not to take it. The time lapse between an incident and when we can speak about it is a variable, but a few days, or even a week, isn't uncommon.

The stimulation in autistic brains is high. (Something to do with a lack of synaptic pruning [possibly!]) To us, the neurotypical world is chaotic, and this leads to the overwhelm I referred to before. Our highly active brains experience the world with the sound turned up. Not just the sound, either. All the senses can be affected, and in true autistic style, this can work the other way too. Compared to neurotypicals, our senses can be less reactive. It's when magnified sensory experiences affect us that neurotypicals struggle the most to relate, but they also assume we're cold when our sensory reactions are less than theirs.

The five senses: sound, sight, touch, taste and smell can all be affected. The form the effect can take will vary from autist to autist and by varying degrees, but usually, we'll all have some sort of sensitivity. What follows are suggestions of the type of sensory issues we may experience. It's unlikely that all of them will affect every autist, but it can happen. Likewise, I've probably missed a few because they don't affect me personally and I've not heard of them affecting others, but I've tried to give as broad an overview as possible.

Sound, for example, is very common. Sensitivities to sound can include things like loud noises such as shouting, laughing, banging, car alarms, screaming children, power tools, even being addressed by our own name when we're not expecting it. Appreciation of the effect loud noises can have on us may be easy, but noises don't have to be loud. Whistling, humming, barely there singing, clicking, tapping, a dripping tap; these can all affect us on a scale that ranges from unsettling, through to creating significant anxiety and even, sometimes, causing actual physical pain. If the duration of the sound is brief, we can usually recover quickly, but if it persists for any length of time, it can overwhelm us.

Autistic people commonly put their hands over their ears to shut out noises that are having an adverse effect on them. If they've faced criticism for over-reacting in the past, they may appear more stoic. However, the tension will be visible in both their faces and taut bodies. To reduce the chance of being affected by noise, many autistic people favour noise-cancelling headphones, or if they like music, regular headphones may do. Drowning out the offending noise with one that's pleasant is also an effective way of removing the source of discomfort.

Auditory Processing Disorder is a common co-morbidity that can affect autistic people. I suspect I may be one of them. If I'm in a noisy environment, I lose the ability to separate sounds. It's like all the noise blobs into one big noise and no single sound is discernible. I need people to look directly at me when speaking to me in these environments, or to make sure they have my attention before speaking, otherwise I may not know they've spoken. Likewise, I may not know that someone is talking to me if I'm concentrating and have dropped into hyper-focus. Both scenarios can lead people to accuse me of ignoring them when I haven't.

I need people to speak clearly or I may not catch everything that's being said and will often need to ask the speaker to repeat themselves. On the phone, I need to focus intently when listening to people because I can't see their face. This is especially true if they speak fast, because that can cause me not to discern any of their words. I Love action films, but can't always follow the dialogue because of all the bangs, shouts and accompanying music, etc. Controlling volume to a reasonable level can help.

Sensitivity to touch is also common and can take on many forms. Textures can play a big part in this, whether the feel of something repels or draws us. When I was younger, I had a problem with liquid soap; I couldn't bear the slimy feel of it in my hands. It would make me feel extremely tense and the urge to get it off my hands was powerful, but solid soaps are rarely available in workplace washrooms.

A soft fabric can have a soothing effect that calms. Many autistic people don't like being touched by other people and will balk at the suggestion of any hugging, but this can also go the other way. Most wouldn't want someone they don't know hugging them, but they may actively like and need the sensation of pressure that a hug can give.

Weighted blankets have been around for a while and are associated with the autistic community. When I was a young child, they didn't exist, and neither did duvets, but blankets were significantly heavier than duvets. My mother changed my sheets weekly and always tucked them in. I never thought about why I did it, but I would never turn my bedding back before getting into bed. I was a small, skinny child and would slide into bed at night from the top of the bed and then slide back out in the morning. My sister pointed out that it didn't look like I'd slept in my bed by the end of the week because the covers had barely moved. I liked the tightness of it, the feeling of being swaddled and the pressure weighing on my body. But how does this impact on the working environment, I hear you cry? Clothing is the issue.

I also favour fitted, but stretchy, clothing unless the weather is hot. Other autists are the opposite and can only bear to wear loose clothing, finding any contact with their skin aggravating. Labels are another well-known irritant. Many autists will routinely cut the labels out of their clothes or wear their underwear inside-out to eliminate the touch of the seams. I don't cut the labels out unless they're driving me insane, mainly because I've found that the stub left behind can cause more discomfort and irritation than the label. Some manufacturers are now printing the label information directly onto the fabric, and this is brilliant for us. The difference it makes is huge.

Another frequent problem, for women, is bras. The irritation they can cause is off the scale. Neurotypical women can relate to how irritating they can be, so imagine multiplying that by a hundred. They can scratch, pinch and rub against our skin to the point of bringing us to insanity. Thankfully, it's now possible to buy seamless, fastener-free, wire-free bras that are comfortable for daily wear.

The effect clothing can have on autistic people is immense and not something to be under-estimated. How an employer wants a uniform to be worn can sometimes be challenging for autists and this can also extend to office attire. For women, the dress-standard is usually flexible enough for them to work around any issues they may have, but for men who're required to wear a suit, this can be a nightmare. A job they enjoy can become untenable simply because of the expectation to work within the prison of fitted clothes, especially when made from rigid fabrics.

Smells can also affect us more than neurotypicals. Some powerful smells can make us sick. Whether it's over-powering body sprays, perfumes and aftershaves, or what someone is having for their lunch, each autist will have their own list, but the effect smells have on our senses can be incredibly strong. I've experienced a few random smells that affected me, from microwaved soups to a popular alcoholic drink.

Lights are another common problem, specifically bright or flickering lights. Over-head strip lighting in offices can often cause problems. They give me headaches, but facing a window so that natural light enters my eyes relieves this problem. The bright lighting used on cosmetic stands in shops can also cause discomfort to autistic people. I find it overpowering.

Tastes are less likely to be an issue in the workplace, but they can still present a problem for autistic people. Food can be problematic from the position of taste, texture and smell, but is only likely to create a problem in the workplace if someone likes to bring strong-smelling food to work.

The temperature in the working environment could present problems for some. It's quite common for autistic people to have problems regulating their body temperature. The process for doing this starts in the brain and often leads to autistic people overheating with very little effort. I've always struggled with this, but thankfully, not to the point of needing to dive naked into the snow during winter to cool off, which is claimed to have happened.

I did, however, once work in an office where not only was the heating on full, but the other women had fan heaters at their feet, too. It was hell. The office wasn't cold and the heating system was more than sufficient. The fan heaters were just overkill. They were fine, but I was burning from the inside. I'm just glad I didn't have to pay their domestic heating bills.

So, with all these factors that can send us over the edge, how do we survive in a world that isn't designed with our needs in mind? Like anyone else, we learn what helps and change what we can. At home, this is easy because we can control our environment, but it's in the workplace where this may not be possible. Often the changes we need are minor by comparison to the effect they have on our well-being and ability to self-regulate. All it takes to achieve this in the workplace is a willingness to cooperate with us.

Another strange thing about sensory issues, especially after everything I've just said, is that we don't always know how we feel about something straight away. For example, a manager might suggest that they want us to do a job that differs from what we usually do. This could be a positive thing – management has noticed our skills in a particular area and wants to utilise them. The usual question that follows is, 'How do you feel about that?' To which they might receive a blank look or a quiet, 'I don't know.'

We aren't being awkward. We aren't even being negative without wanting to say so. The odds are, we genuinely don't know how we feel about it and need time to process what is being suggested before being able to communicate it. Processing delays are common to autists and feelings aren't always immediately apparent. It can take time for us to figure out how we feel and some autists can't name what they're feeling when the feeling is there.

So, when so many ordinary situations can affect us, how do we handle this? There are several ways to create or restore calm.

Calmly Does It

Many autistic people, and I'm one of them, will confess that home is a sanctuary. It's the one place where we can be ourselves without feeling like we're walking on eggshells and where we can have control over our environment. It's the place we can spend our time doing what interests us without a helpful individual telling us why we should want to do something else, like getting out more, for example. Sadly, most of us can't work from home, but, for the sake of our sanity, many will if they can find a way.

Whether at home or at work, the steps we take to mitigate sensory issues help to calm us and prevent overwhelm. I've already mentioned headphones. These can help us more than any neurotypical could ever appreciate. Finding a space that's free of noise and people who're determined to talk to us when we're trying to centre ourselves is another. Something I haven't mentioned yet is stimming.

Stimming is a self-regulatory behaviour that isn't even unique to autistic people. Neurotypical people do it too, but it's more obvious with autistic people and usually takes a form that's perceived as less socially acceptable than how a neurotypical person would do it.

Stimming can take the form of rocking, swinging a leg, swinging an arm, flapping hands, snapping fingers, twirling, walking on tiptoes, pacing, jumping, foot tapping, pen tapping, twirling or flicking hair, playing with an object, e.g., glasses, pens, a ball, a coaster; basically, anything that's available. Speaking to ourselves or holding a fabric with a calming texture can also help. These things can bring an anxious or stressed person back to a place of equilibrium. Something else that works for autistic people is our interests.

All autists have particular interests. Some of these interests are lifelong and others come and go, but things that interest us hold our attention. Some people call our interests obsessions, but this annoys me. It's an incredibly arrogant interpretation of what drives us. Have you ever heard of anyone who goes out with friends every night being accused of having an obsession with socialising?

I'll accept my interests are obsessions when neurotypical people accept their obsession with social interaction and connection. 'Oh no, no,' they cry, 'that's not an obsession, it's a normal need!' Well, guess what? It may be a normal need for neurotypicals, but autistic people don't need social interaction to the same extent and our interests are a normal need for us.

Eliza Jane Blake

Neurotypicals understand people needing social interaction, but they're distrustful of those who don't, because they can't relate to it. Ergo, what we need is wrong, but what would be the point of living in a state of disinterested isolation?

What would be the point of anybody if they had no desire to fill their time with any type of activity, even if that something is meditating? Labelling us obsessional can be offensive. Our interests energise us and focus our thoughts on a single task. They calm us in a world that unsettles us. Neurotypical people do what interests and relaxes them every time they meet up with friends. Their social outings energise and calm them. Great! We get why they want to do that, but the understanding doesn't work both ways.

We aren't being selfish when we don't want to attend social functions or can only stay for a limited time. And why do work parties always involve bringing a partner? They don't work there! Putting aside that many (but not all) autists are single, it's an added pressure that ultimately increases our isolation; either because we're there alone or because we choose not to go, which is interpreted as a rejection of spending time with our colleagues. It's a cruel expectation, selfish, even, and the worse thing is when those insisting we go know they're being cruel, but it entertains them to put us in that situation.

Accusations of being weird or obsessional about our interests can extend beyond activities. Sometimes, autistic people stand accused of being obsessional about other people. Maybe there is some truth to this for some, but in my experience, the people I'm drawn to are the ones who have friendly personas, don't sneer and don't treat me any differently than anyone else. Do I prefer to be around people like that? Of course I do.

Unfortunately, the easy and lazy explanation is that I have an obsessional interest. Neurotypical people can't understand why anyone would prefer to limit their contact to a few or just one person unless that interest has an ulterior motive. I hope that having read the book so far, other explanations might make more sense.

Remember the chapter about social interaction? Consider the limited ability to read faces and body language and how I can read the obvious expressions but am lost in nuance? If someone is smiling at me, to a degree at least, I can relax, but if someone is giving me that blank, unreadable look that I'm clearly supposed to understand but don't, then I'm not feeling comfortable.

When people are trying to manipulate me, I can't relax, especially once I've realised they're the sort of person who would indulge in that behaviour either for entertainment or to take advantage. Then there's the sneering. What's that about? Apart from knowing that I'm being judged negatively, I still don't know why they're doing it.

So, to come full circle, I need to feel calm and that means being relaxed. Without that, I have no hope of self-regulation because my anxiety levels will rise, resulting in stress. The people I gravitate towards are those who don't make me nervous. It's as simple as that. They're the people who allow me to be who I am without judgement or condescension; people who're open and friendly to others without discrimination. People who're safe for me to relax around rather than feel compelled to remain wary and hypervigilant.

Eliza Jane Blake

Neurotypical social interaction is what we struggle with, particularly in group settings. This is the difference or disability. There's no big secret. No big crush. No need for all the gossip and speculation that neurotypicals love to indulge in so much. Neurotypicals routinely reject autists because we're different and misunderstood. It's not much of a stretch to recognise that we're going to be drawn to the friendly people who don't do that to us.

Being able to relax is important and our interests provide us with essential relief. When we focus on the activities or topics that interest us, we can relax. It calms our hyperactive brains. Rather than having multiple thoughts rampaging through our minds and multiple sensory inputs overwhelming us and causing discomfort; all the thoughts, questions, doubts and memories clamouring for our time, retreat. Our brains focus on just that which is in front of us and it's the closest we can get to peace. It's the quietest our brains can be. By dropping into hyper-focus or hyper-fixation, we can enjoy whatever we're doing without the chaos of the outside world triggering our brains.

Hyper-focus and hyper-fixation are states of intense concentration. When we're at work, we don't drop into these states intentionally and rarely realise that we have, but it's a sign that we're enjoying our work and feel comfortable doing it. Hyper-fixation is usually associated with our hobbies and interests, while hyper-focus is task specific and of a shorter duration. The best thing about being in hyper-focus, apart from how productive we can be, is that while in this state, we're less aware of our environment. More accurately, our environment isn't unsettling or harming us. All the noise has retreated to a soundproof box deep in our brain. We're calm and the peace is fantastic. At least, until someone decides we've been quiet for too long and yanks us out of it.

It's often when we're in this state that people accuse us of ignoring them. We're not, we just haven't heard them or been aware of them. Forcing us out of hyper-focus shocks our brains and takes a while to reorient from. It's like being woken from a deep sleep by someone shaking us. The wake-up is brutal. It's when we're dragged out of this state that we may not react kindly to being interrupted and may have problems 'shifting gears' or changing direction.

Unfortunately, neurotypicals often haul us out of this state because they want us to do something else instead, or they interpret our lack of interaction as rudeness or inappropriate. Essentially, the perception is that we're not meeting the needs of others, or we're isolating ourselves from the group. It helps to allow us to focus on a task through to completion rather than allow us to immerse in a task only to drag us away from it prematurely because, besides breaking our concentration, we can also find it difficult to concentrate on anything for some time afterwards. We're not being awkward. It's a reflection of how unsettled and disoriented we are.

Dropping into hyper-focus is a consequence of our brain function. It's not a personal rejection and we don't feel like we're missing out for not being present. As I mentioned earlier, we don't even realise when we're dropping into it, but rather than being a sign of boredom or dislike of others in the room, it's a sign that we're enjoying what we're doing.

It's also this propensity to sink into a deep concentration that can cause time blindness. We often won't notice the passing of time when we're engrossed. This can apply both in the workplace and at home. We're never late on purpose. In fact, autistic people are rarely late for actual appointments. When we know we must be somewhere, we'll usually be early and will diligently take steps to ensure we don't mess up. Being late is too stressful, so we're often early.

Autistic people are likely to experience health issues throughout their lives as a direct consequence of living in a neurotypical world, whether because of the expectations that are placed upon us by others or the chaotic environments we have to navigate. I mentioned earlier how suicide rates are higher within the autistic community than in the general population. This needs to stop and I hope that by reaching out to employers, managers, trainers and everybody who works in the many organisations around the world, we can achieve this.

Ignoring autistic needs has consequences, not only for the autist, but for those around them. 'Meltdown' is a much-misused term now, but ignoring it isn't an option either. We might as well confront it directly.

Stress is the Limit

Autistic people can experience high levels of stress in the workplace as a direct consequence of the expectations, assumptions, nastiness and disciplinary procedures we're so often subjected to. This is on top of the stress we experience because of sensory issues and misunderstandings surrounding communication differences, not to mention the stresses experienced by everybody in the work environment. It's often the inability or limited ability to handle stress that leads to those plots to oust us.

An inability to control stress is a key trait connected with autistic brain function. It's this that can lead to meltdowns or, what I prefer to call, autistic venting. Whatever we call it, this predictable expression of stress is neither laziness nor poor behaviour on our part. This trait is also a consequence of our brain chemistry.

Eliza Jane Blake

It's neither a character flaw nor a personality defect and isn't something neurotypicals should expect autistic people to have neurotypical-grade control over. The common response is to punish us when we can't contain it, but listening, once we're able to talk, is the appropriate response and this may take a while.

Bear with me while I duck the onslaught of indignation erupting around me! Yes, I know these seemingly inappropriate outbursts can be unsettling, offensive and upsetting to those caught in the crossfire, but I also know how upsetting they are for the autistic person who feels like their head just exploded. In truth, the escalation in stress levels happens so fast, it's virtually impossible to intercept without a lot of help and training, which means an early diagnosis and intervention, and even then, there's no guarantee the autist will recognise the signs in time to remove themselves from the source of the stress.

I'm aware there are autistic people who say they can control their stress levels and maybe that's true if they've had help from tolerant adults when they were children, but I suspect avoidance of triggers has more to do with it and that's not the same thing. It is, however, good news for neurotypicals in the workplace. By understanding, recognising and controlling triggers, we can reduce, if not eliminate, instances of autistic venting.

There are so many potential triggers it's impossible for me to highlight them all. The best thing an employer can do is to ask the individual autist. However, please be aware, we might not know them all and will only realise that something needs to be added to our list once it's triggered us. I can, however, offer a starting point. External stress caused by information or sensory overload will play a part.

Each puts an autist's brain under more stress and their brain will seek a way to ease the stress if it becomes too much. Please note, I said the brain will seek relief, not the person. That wasn't an over-sight and it's an important distinction to make. Autistic venting isn't a choice; it's an act of self-protection. The autist's brain is trying to relieve the pressure by expelling the stress to restore equilibrium.

The term 'meltdown' annoys me immensely because the person who coined it did nothing to distinguish it from what it's erroneously assumed to be: a tantrum. Hence, why I prefer autistic venting. To be clear, this release of stress isn't a tantrum. Tantrums are deliberate and manipulative ploys, usually engaged by a child, to persuade their caregivers to provide them with what they want after they've been told they can't have something. Autistic venting, by comparison, is involuntary. It's a temporary loss of control. For most autistic adults, it's never violent, even if it's loud and looks scary. It isn't even necessarily a demonstration of anger. Ventings are caused by overwhelm and a struggle to control our emotions can present as any powerful emotion. When people are upset, anger or tears are common reactions for us all.

So, autistic venting is a release of stress caused by a source of overwhelm. As I mentioned earlier, different factors can contribute to the stress, but a sensory issue or information overload will play a part. Uncertainty can also contribute. (Remember all those questions we ask in the search for clarity?) Autists need certainty like neurotypicals need social contact, and both confusion and uncertainty can cause an escalation of stress levels.

Eliza Jane Blake

Having too much to think about in one go will cause a rapid rise in stress levels. Being under time pressure can create or add to it. Being accused of things we don't recognise to be true is another and that's on top of the sensory issues. Underestimating the effect of sensory issues should never happen, but that they are, explains many of the problems. The important thing to remember about stress and autistic brain function is that our stress levels are rarely low by comparison to neurotypical brains because we're being affected by sensory stimulation most of the time. Therefore, when stress rises – and in our case, this is a rapid escalation – we're starting from a point that's already higher than most people.

I should also point out that when an autistic adult experiences a venting episode, it's likely that more than one trigger is involved. It's the compounded effect. First one trigger, then before we've recovered from that, another one happens, and if it gets to three, boom! We can't cope. It's this that can often make it seem like the reaction has come from nowhere, because when the cause is a compounded effect, each trigger can be small and seemingly insignificant.

Our brains are noisy. By that, I mean that our brains rarely stop thinking in multiple directions because of the high stimulation I mentioned before. Because of this, dropping into hyper-focus can be helpful for us. Our thoughts are like hyperactive gymnasts, spinning and flipping through our brains, unless our focus can lock onto a single direction. Hyperactivity can relate to brain function as well as physical movement. Some autists aren't physically hyperactive at all – many are the most unathletic people you will ever meet – but some of us are. Personally, I'm both physically and mentally hyperactive.

Smash The Boulder

None of us want to be in situations where we've become overwhelmed. We know only too well how difficult neurotypicals find these flashes of release, but what we wish neurotypicals also knew was first how to prevent them and second how to respond to them appropriately, because often, neurotypical action or expectation unintentionally causes or escalates them. Avoidance of these undesirable outbursts is relatively simple, but we need neurotypical cooperation.

We need help to control the environment to avoid triggers: noise, temperature, smells, lighting, clothing requirements, space and proximity to other people. Too many demands can overwhelm us – this doesn't mean instructions can't be front-loaded, just allow us the time to write them down, or better still, send them by email if the working environment allows.

Gossiping about us causes stress. When there's something people want to know, ask us, rather debating with each other and making inaccurate assumptions. Be patient and answer our questions. We need clarity so we can proceed with confidence. Everybody has strengths and weaknesses, including neurotypicals, so try not to be judgemental about our limitations.

Cooperating with us to minimise known triggers will help, but sometimes a grenade flies in unexpectedly and takes everybody by surprise. In these situations, there's a right and a wrong way to react to autistic venting. The good news is the right way is much simpler than you may realise.

To make this easy, I'm going to go out on a limb and state that there's a right and a wrong way to deal with a child's tantrum. Yes, I know I said that autistic venting isn't a tantrum, but stay with me, because while they're inherently different, the way to deal with them is the same. The right way is simply to walk away. When a child is deliberately trying to manipulate their caregiver into caving in, showing them it won't work is the way to deal with it and stop it happening in the future. There's no need to shout, judge or mock, just walk away. Do that and the child will quickly learn they're wasting their time.

Autistic venting is different in that it's neither deliberate nor manipulative, but it needs to play out to get it out. Don't react or respond, don't take it personally, but also don't judge that the person should know better than this; we aren't neurotypical and wouldn't be considered disabled if our experiences matched that of the majority. Likewise, once the release has passed, don't come back with loaded words such as, 'do you feel better now?' Or, 'have you done now?' Or worse, 'is it safe to speak to you now?' The last thing an autistic person needs is to be patronised. We already feel far worse than anybody else in the room. The only other thing that would help us is to remove or reduce the source of the distress.

The wrong way to deal with autistic venting, or a tantrum for that matter, is to confront it. When anybody does that, they become part of the problem because they're adding to the stress the person's brain is trying to release. When people confront it, they enter the realm of deciding this person needs to learn and they're going to teach them. They've allowed their own ego to get in the way. As I pointed out earlier, it's the person's brain that's trying to release the stress, not the person. When people try to intervene and control what's happening to me during a venting, the consequence is usually a shutdown.

Most people know autists can be non-speaking, but it's not so well known that speaking autists can become non-speaking in certain circumstances. This is one of them. When a person tries to intervene to stop a venting instead of letting it play out, the increase in stress, rather than the reduction of it, sends my brain into shutdown to protect itself. I can no longer speak or respond. People assume I'm now sulking, but I wasn't having a tantrum and the reason I'm no longer speaking is that I can't. Some autists also find themselves unable to physically move when their brain goes into shutdown.

Thankfully, this is quite rare in the workplace and the good news is that when we control the sources of overwhelm, we also control the likelihood of a venting. They don't have to happen, but only if people are open to working with us to provide autistic-friendly working environments and that shouldn't be any great hardship.

This means being aware of the factors I've already listed. Things like sensory triggers: smells, noises and artificial lights can all contribute to the overwhelm. Putting requests for tasks to be done in the autist's notebook or sending them via email rather than giving verbal instructions. Just having tasks written rather than whirling around inside our heads can massively reduce stress and overwhelm. Being aware of our differences in communication style and aiming for clarity. It may take a while to get the hang of being aware of when assumptions are being made, but even if it proves too difficult to avoid them, at least it should be possible to recognise where any misunderstandings have originated from. Be as direct as possible.

Autistic people consider directness a gift of rare value. Don't be hesitant to use it. Even if the words sting initially, it won't last for long and we'd rather know where we stand than try to figure out subtext – a process that's extremely stressful and confusing for us.

Another way managers can put unnecessary stress onto autistic people is by assuming that we need hounding to do our work. Autistic people are extremely productive, especially when at work. It would be highly unlikely that an autist would need anyone leaning over their shoulder, cajoling them to get on with the job. Interpersonal skills might be the neurotypical forte, but productivity is where autists excel and we rarely get sidetracked by talking.

We'll never instinctively have the soft skills neurotypicals respect, but autists are the most productive workers you'll ever employ. This is our holy grail, if you like. Unfortunately, because neurotypicals rate interpersonal skills so highly (the arena they naturally excel in) all too often, they use the skill that sets autists apart, against us. They dismiss the benefits of our productivity as insignificant.

Neurotypicals want to talk to each other and sometimes need a nudge to pull them back on track. But it annoys us that management tolerates their 'lack' with a smile (because this is normal behaviour to be expected) when they rarely tolerate our perceived shortcomings.

The misunderstandings surrounding autistic traits lead to blatant discrimination in the workplace. It's illegal in the United Kingdom to discriminate against anybody because of their disability, yet many employers use vetting questionnaires to weed out undesirable applicants before they even get an interview. The focus is on finding applicants with those all-important interpersonal skills: being a team player, being laid back and approachable, or unflappable. If you've read the book so far, you know what I'm getting at.

Smash The Boulder

Many autists would fail these tests. However, if an autist is intelligent and has been surviving in this neurotypical world long enough, we can know what the right answers are before filling them in. Even more relevant, we aren't playing the system like you'd imagine. Essentially, we are that sought after person – until overwhelm kicks in or we communicate something in the 'wrong' way.

The other thing about autists is our inherent honesty. Contrary to what many neurotypicals like to believe, most of us are kind people who care deeply about our fellow humans. Neurotypicals often accuse us of lacking empathy, but not only is this accusation untrue, but autistic people also recognise this lack in most neurotypical people. We don't feel that we receive much empathy.

Autistic venting is a classic example of cause and effect in action. There's always a cause; a trigger is a better word, but regardless of whether neurotypicals can see it, the trigger is always there. We need to work together to eliminate or reduce them. We need neurotypicals to understand that things that don't affect them may well affect us.

That neurotypicals can't relate to our reality, doesn't alter the situation, or justify ignoring it because it's too much like hard work. This needs to be accepted, and a willingness adopted to work with us to control the environment. Autistic people have endured the discomfort of neurotypical environments for a long time. Meeting us half-way shouldn't be too much to ask.

Once upon a time, businesses favoured individual offices to promote productivity. Some time ago, managers discarded this approach and replaced it with open-plan offices and an encouragement to interact with each other. Autists accept this works for neurotypical people, but we ask employers to consider it may make some workplaces no-go zones for some autistic people, unless they're prepared to make whatever minor adjustments autistic people need to make the environment more tolerable.

Autistic ventings are hard to witness, we know this. We know how powerful they are and how disconcerting and unsettling they can be. But they're no fun for us either. The assumption that we should have more control over our emotions is based on neurotypical standards, but our brains don't work like theirs.

Would anybody find ventings so hard to forgive if they knew none of it was about them and the person struggling is releasing frustration and stress in the only way their brain can?

Remember, the correct response is to walk away. Anybody can do that. Squash the urge to intervene, knowing that when left alone, the moment will pass much faster. Judgements, taking personal offense, demanding retribution; none of it helps anybody.

'But we shouldn't have to tolerate it!' 'Have some consideration for others!' We know this is how neurotypicals feel about them, but venting isn't a choice and no one is choosing to disrupt anyone's peace. An eruption may feel personal, but isn't. Please let me repeat that. Venting isn't personal. Nor does it represent a character flaw or a personality defect. We don't want to be venting any more than neurotypicals want to witness it.

Autistic people find many of the things neurotypicals do inconsiderate, whether it's trying to force us to be sociable when we need distance, creating sensory triggers, expecting us to understand hints and around-about ways of communicating, or expecting us to read their faces when we have no clue what it is we're expected to understand or know. We don't enjoy venting either, but when we can't control our environment and others won't work with us to manage our needs, choice doesn't come into it.

If our brains didn't release the pressure, we'd implode. We vehemently wish we could avoid it, but all too often, the stress mounts quicker than we can intervene to stop it. The shame that's heaped upon us, both by those around us and ourselves, is likely a contributory factor to the higher instances of suicide among the autistic population. Kindness and a willingness to work with us can reduce the stress we struggle to cope with.

Hand in hand with heightened stress levels is anxiety. The levels of anxiety we experience just trying to exist in the neurotypical world with its loud noises, smells, uncomfortable clothing, social expectations and vague communication style are high enough, but the expected risk of tripping up or causing offense to others by saying or doing the wrong thing and the consequences that will automatically follow, takes it to a whole other level that's on a par with the anxiety people living with an abusive partner experience. Please don't assume I'm trivialising the reality of the abused because I'm not. Our anxiety levels reach these heights.

The fear and sense of walking on eggshells hoping that we don't inadvertently make a mistake resulting in punishment, or worse, lose our job and the financial security that's inherently connected to it, is an enormous burden to carry through life.

Eliza Jane Blake

The financial potential of autistic people is often limited because of unrealistic expectations being placed upon them and our self-esteem takes regular beatings because of how others react to us and the punishments people feel justified in inflicting upon us.

Many of us find our confidence to take on mortgages can be severely affected because of the fear about financial stability resulting from misunderstandings in the workplace and the higher risk we face of being subjected to disciplinary procedures because of our disability (regardless of the existence of a diagnosis). This is assuming we aren't under-employed to the point where we can only find minimum wage jobs that don't reflect our intellectual abilities and don't provide an income sufficient to allow a mortgage to be granted.

When it's considered that so many of us are doing this on our own, without a support network or partner should the worst happen, essentially without a safety net, this anxiety can be especially acute. Because of the problems we can face forming relationships, many autistic people face these realities alone. It's no wonder autistic people are more likely to experience problems with depression throughout their lives and are statistically more likely to end their life by suicide than neurotypicals.

I've walked this tightrope as a single parent. Over time, the hypervigilance so many autists cling to in the name of survival, malfunctions. Our self-worth erodes to the point of destruction and, ultimately, becomes a burden that's just too heavy to carry. Is it really any wonder masking causes burnout throughout our lives, but especially once we get past forty? The energy it takes to live a lie is huge and simply isn't sustainable throughout a working lifetime, which at the moment, is being extended every few years, it seems.

Now put that into the context of the workplace. People have enough to think about at work already: customers, demanding bosses, workload, time pressures, office politics. Imagine the stress of trying to juggle the usual balls on top of trying to deny inherent brain function to fit in with peers and stay out of trouble.

We have to mind our words and how we say them, stay aware of the expression on our faces, avoid dropping into hyper-focus (even though that's the most productive state to be in at work) so we don't inadvertently ignore someone, take part in small talk we have no interest in and try to understand the neurotypical way of communicating without making any mistakes. Not to mention the sensory issues. It's too much, and yet, we often face accusations of not trying hard enough. For many, it's more than we can cope with and so we either find a way of working from home or we don't work at all and then we're considered a burden on society; lazy, perfectly capable of working but choosing not to. It's soul destroying.

Most autistic people want to work and are more than capable of doing so. But the stress of having to juggle everything at once is simply too much, especially if we're trying to do it on our own. Is it too much to ask for us to be allowed to be our true selves at work? Many employers now say that we should all be able to do that and some are actively asking their employees if they feel able to bring their true selves to work. But few have educated themselves on neurodiversity or educated their employees about what it can look like. Maybe this is because the information hasn't been available in a concise, easily readable form. I hope this book has changed that.

Reasonable adjustments are the only realistic solution for creating an environment we can all comfortably work in, but that means us all cooperating to make it happen. No judgement. No resentment of perceived special treatment. Reasonable adjustments merely create an environment that we can comfortably work in, just as neurotypicals do every day, and it only needs a willingness to make each other's lives better to make that happen.

It may be a game of trial and error to establish exactly what it is in any working environment that causes an autistic person to overload, but we can identify it and take steps to minimise the chances of overload happening again – but only if employers will work with us rather than run us out of the building.

I just have one more thing to say about stress and how it affects us and that's the irony that we can handle situations that neurotypicals can't cope with. It's true. Consider it the ultimate contradiction. The big stuff, the things that make neurotypicals scream, cry and tear their hair out, are the things that autists calmly take in their stride.

In direct contrast to what I've been talking about in this chapter, neurotypicals also often criticise us for being too emotionless. I dispute the allegation, although it's certainly true we experience our emotions differently and may hold more inside in some respects. But autists are usually logical thinkers. We approach practical problems with a logical mindset rather than an emotional one.

So, when the roof literally caves in, the autist will deal with it rather than fall apart. When the neurotypicals around us

Smash The Boulder

can't think straight, we're the ones with the cool head doing what needs to be done. A fact for which we can still expect criticism because neurotypicals can't relate to how we can hold it all together, given the circumstances. In fact, it could be argued, it's a miracle we're able to function at all when our health takes such a battering from day to day.

Sick and Tired

We all wear masks. Anyone who's tried to make a good impression, whether during a job interview or in the early days of a new relationship, knows what it is to wear a mask. But autistic masking is a pretence on another level and it takes a tremendous amount of energy to do it successfully. When I joined my last employer, I had no choice but to bring my true self to work. I was so run down I didn't have the energy to fake anything.

For autists, masking involves hiding our instinctive brain function. It's a denial of who we really are and the price we're expected to pay for acceptance. We must sustain the pretence all day, every day. One slip and the assumption is that we're behaving badly out of choice. After all, we're intelligent and we know how to behave properly – we prove it all the time. But consistency is everything.

Smash The Boulder

Over time, the pretence becomes harder to achieve and without this ability, autistic people sink. Any instance of overwhelm, caused by whatever trigger, interrupts the direction of our energy and our resolve to uphold the façade can collapse in an instant. When it does, our best intentions count for nothing.

Society's lack of awareness about autistic brain function is so complete, without a diagnosis, we're condemned and left to drown. The very nature of authentic autistic traits is why it can be so damaging for us to bring our true selves to work. The punishments quickly follow. When I couldn't mask and had no choice but to bring my true self to work, I soon remembered why I'd been wearing a mask (albeit a slightly transparent and wonky mask) for all those years.

The gossip, the assumptions, the bitching, the judging, it was horrific and on the back of it all, my stress levels went sky high and we all know how bad for our health stress is, particularly when prolonged.

Humour me, just for a moment, and imagine that for one week, you've got to communicate the autistic way. No subtext, no hints, a direct manner and everything you see and hear interpreted in a literal way. Add to that, having to pretend that you can only read people's faces and body language in a limited way and that your brain might experience processing delays. Your senses will also react to stimuli in your environment you've never been aware of before.

Imagine the lights ten times brighter, every loud sound reverberating in your head, every powerful smell making you want to be physically sick, and every crowd literally closing in on you, making you want to look to the floor and run in the opposite direction. Imagine the confusion of knowing that people are thinking something negative about you, but not knowing what or why. Imagine the need to reflect quietly on your own thoughts, while others constantly try to draw you away from them. Imagine everything you do and say being condemned as wrong, including your feelings, interpretations, and priorities. Do you think you could pull it off? Do you think you could survive it?

Now imagine you've got to sustain the pretence for a month, or a year, or a lifetime. At no time can you be your true self and if you do, any perceived deviation from the expected standard will lead to punishment.

This is the reality autistic people face in the workplace every day; particularly if they aren't aware of their neurotype. The drain on our energy is relentless and ultimately leads to burnout.

Autistic burnout is a debilitating state that results in physical fatigue, compromised concentration, elusive motivation, memory issues and a general inability to function effectively. It's directly caused by too much masking. And this is the reason recognition of autistic traits needs to be commonplace.

Masking is bad for our health, but the only way we can stop doing it is if society learns to recognise the autistic neurotype and is open to accepting our differences.

We don't want to reach a point where burnout destroys what we've built, but it's a real risk as we get older, whether because a lack of energy has taken our motivation, or because we've had enough of the demands and expectations of others and want to live a life that suits us, rather than everyone else.

Smash The Boulder

Ironically, those autistic people who can control their rising stress levels to prevent any venting are probably the most likely to experience burnout in the long-term. Particularly if they're suppressing who they really are rather than reducing and avoiding triggers.

Autistic children, without intellectual impairment, are often taught how to control their responses to stimuli and learn neurotypical social rules. The bias towards fitting in is supposed to help them avoid being bullied for their differences. The teaching is also heavily biased towards letting the autistic child know how their behaviour affects others. They're taught how important it is to consider the feelings of others, and by that, I mean how neurotypicals feel. It would be a good thing to receive the same consideration, but we don't.

It's an old-school practice where neurotypicals assume their way is the right way and autists learn that we're not normal (even if that isn't how it's sold to us) and the burden to fit in rests upon us. This practice, in the long run, not only harms the autist, but releases neurotypicals from any responsibility to regulate their own behaviour or expectations. Historically, as the majority, they've had no obligation to accommodate others because they're not faulty (in their eyes). How they are is 'normal' and the onus is on those who're different to do all the bending.

Until now, masking has been the only way for autistic people to survive in neurotypical workplaces. Unfortunately, many autistic people either can't mask at all or can't do so consistently.

Teaching autistic children to control their impulses and responses is teaching them how to mask. Even teaching them how to avoid triggers to protect themselves from overwhelm, can only work when they have control over their environment, which they rarely do at school and later in the workplace, without supportive managers and coworkers.

The only way to protect autistic people from the fate of burnout is for them to live in a world where they don't have to pretend to be someone they're not and where they don't have to deny how their brains work.

To be clear, I'm not advocating a reality where autists have no responsibility. I want an understanding of our differences, from both neurotypes, to minimise misunderstandings and stop autistic people being punished for not being neurotypical.

Consideration can only work both ways if both neurotypes are aware of the differences. The price for our health is too high to continue ignoring it, because as debilitating as burnout can be, there are other consequences for our health, too.

We can all mitigate some things easily. For example, a recognition that autists would rather communicate in writing because of struggles with verbal communication. But even the NHS often insists on contacting us by phone when we'd prefer an email or text. The same applies to therapy services that insist on face-to-face contact. When health services don't accommodate our communication needs, it's clear to see what we're up against. Most autists won't answer their phones when they don't know who's calling. It's too stressful. If their phone doesn't have the caller's name saved in its memory, or it's a withheld number, the caller will only connect to voicemail and the autist may not receive vital information.

Another example of how health services and governments don't prioritise our needs is how long we have to wait for assessments. The wait was long before Covid, but now it's three times longer than before the lockdowns. The anxiety of not knowing, combined with the risk of facing disciplinary action or losing our jobs, is too easy to ignore or downplay by a health service facing stretched budgets.

Societies have made big strides in recent years to understand the importance of mental health, but little has changed to services, despite the known connection between mental and physical health.

There are conditions that can afflict autistic people which others can't help us avoid, but an awareness of them can help prevent some misunderstandings.

Autistic people seem more likely to contract autoimmune diseases. A common comorbidity for those with autistic brains is an autoimmune disease that affects the thyroid (also known as Hashimoto's disease). In the UK, the doctor I consulted only referred to it as an underactive thyroid, but this doesn't explain what's happening. Specifically, a person's antibodies attack their thyroid gland, causing damage. This condition isn't unique to autistic people and often runs in families, but the incidence seems to be much higher for autists than in the general population.

Diagnosis often only occurs after a significant amount of damage has been done. But left untreated, this can cause depression among other symptoms, or in our case, significantly add to a depression that's already there. The hormone, thyroxine, which is produced by the thyroid gland, is involved in the distribution of energy to the body's organs – including the brain – and it's this physical aspect that causes depression when the brain isn't receiving enough energy to function properly. Other common symptoms include stiff joints, weight gain and tiredness. Unfortunately, few people know how to recognise the symptoms of depression, let alone the other aspects, but a broader awareness in the workplace would thwart inaccurate assumptions about affected colleagues, regardless of whether they're autistic.

I'm aware this thyroid condition also seems quite prevalent within the ADHD community, too, and ADHD is itself another common comorbidity associated with being autistic. OCD (Obsessive Compulsive Disorder) is another, although autistic people can appear to have OCD traits anyway as part of being autistic. This is because of the autistic need for routine and sameness - another tendency for which we can expect ridicule.

Our sensory issues often lead to problems with anxiety. When we're young, it can often feel like we don't know what will hijack us around the next corner and as children, we struggle to deal with the uncertainty. This feeling often persists into adulthood.

Even without Hashimoto's disease, depression is a common comorbidity for autistic people. I take medication for clinical depression and it helps enormously, but I don't believe this condition has developed because I'm autistic. Its roots stem back to anxiety, an anxiety that's accompanied me through every step of my life. At its heart is a fear of doing wrong combined with knowing that no matter how hard I try not to, I'll still be wrong according to others and I can expect to be punished for not meeting their expectations. It can be about anything, big or small, but I know judgement and punishment will find me. They always have.

Consider the aftermath of an autistic venting in the workplace. The person on the receiving end of any explosion is feeling aggrieved. They're nursing a bruised ego for which they hold the autist solely responsible. This person wants retribution. They want to see the one with the inability to control their emotions punished and everybody around them agrees: such appalling behaviour! Everybody has empathy for the one with the bruised ego.

By comparison, everyone has nothing but contempt for the autist. Worse than that, the autist, who may not even know they're autistic, has nothing but contempt for themselves. Just for a moment, take a step back and put yourself in the autist's shoes. Imagine the feeling of shame and hating yourself as much as everybody else does. The knowing that it's always your fault. Imagine how we feel when we walk into work again and face everybody.

Imagine receiving the looks, the contempt, the sneers, the mocking or silent treatment. Can you imagine the strength it takes to do that, not just once in your life, but repeatedly? When people decide to punish, there's no kindness. Even worse for us is knowing those punishments won't change a single thing.

Even if we have a diagnosis, we can't change our brain chemistry. In the right circumstances, it will happen again. Those who don't have a diagnosis don't know why they can't control their emotions. Indeed, in their eyes, their outburst was justified – cause and effect. If they've never received a diagnosis, they've had no support and no explanation for what happened or why things affect them, but don't have the same effect on others.

People have often told me I'm overreacting, but my emotions are what they are. Nobody has the right to tell another the way they feel is wrong or that their feelings don't matter, but there's no empathy where there's no relating or understanding.

If the cause of the venting is environmental or some other sensory issue, even knowing the cause won't stop it from happening again because we need cooperation from others to control the environment which few accept, because they can't relate to the affect it has on us. Even if they do, many object to making accommodations for the comfort of one.

Except it wouldn't be for the comfort of one, because controlling the environment would be in everyone's interests. But in the eyes of the world, if everyone else can control themselves, there's no excuse for those who can't. It must be that we aren't trying hard enough and so the world continues to punish us until we make the required effort to control our emotions. That neurotypicals think it's so easy, makes us feel even worse and the fact that it will never be easy for us, is a kick in the teeth.

Controlling the environment and minimising known triggers can prevent autistic venting, but removal of those triggers won't happen without a willingness to work with us and unfortunately, there are many posts on social media within the autistic community that show a reluctance by neurotypical employers to do this. Why should anyone accommodate 'fussiness' when it's easier to dispense with the autist and hire somebody else? While company policies dictate autistic traits are unacceptable, management feels confident to dispense with undesirables on this basis.

So, the health of autistic people continues to decline because people don't want the inconvenience of accommodating us. We're assumed high maintenance, but respect and consideration are two-way processes. Society shouldn't put all the responsibility on us – the ones labelled with a disorder and considered disabled. Society knows it can't exclude people in wheelchairs and neither should it exclude us.

It's not right to assume that we're bad or don't care. We care very much. We also wish this world didn't overwhelm us, but it's not designed with us in mind. It's designed by neurotypicals for neurotypicals; people who, from where we stand, demand respect and consideration from us, but don't give it back.

There are some who believe that a cure for autistic brain function is the solution – not to improve autistic lives, but to protect neurotypical lives from being blighted by our existence. They believe we're such an offensive abomination they shouldn't have to exist alongside us.

These are the people who accuse us of selfishness, while believing their own needs must come before anybody else's and that they shouldn't have to make any compromises. So, who are the selfish, self-serving ones? Who is it that lacks empathy and flexibility?

Most autistic people don't want to be cured. Our brains function exceptionally well in most respects, and how our brains work is normal to us. If neurotypicals think we lack empathy, we can say the same. We don't see faultless human beings any more than we believe we're perfect. It would be easier if we did – at least then the contempt would be justified.

For us, work is usually fine until overwhelm strikes. Just one venting episode is enough for all previous opinions of us to be relegated to the 'think again' bin. From that moment on, we're treated with contempt by everyone around us with any chance of progressing within the organisation gone and we end up wanting to leave as much as our neurotypical colleagues hope we will.

We can be the funniest around until a venting occurs, then we're not funny at all. Now we're treated with mistrust, like we're the wolf in Grandma's clothing. Is it any wonder that so many of us end up fighting with depression – bearing in mind that clinical depression isn't just about emotions and feelings, it's a physical illness? Brain function becomes sluggish. Depressed people become physically slower of movement. How is a brain that isn't working at the correct speed supposed to not only have the energy to prevent venting episodes when we struggle under normal circumstances, but to maintain the intense focus needed to wear a mask?

A nervousness can follow us through life, particularly if punishments or ridicule followed our responses and reactions when we were children. This often leads to resentment, defensiveness and hypervigilance as adults.

Most people have heard of PTSD (Post Traumatic Stress Disorder) but not so many have heard of CPTSD (Complex Post Traumatic Stress Disorder). A single traumatic event is usually responsible for PTSD. A combination of extended exposure to stressful events or the occurrence of multiple stressful events, compounded, can cause CPTSD. Research seems to suggest autistic people are significantly more likely to develop PTSD than the neurotypical population. (See the National Autistic Society's website for more detailed information.)

Is it any surprise that drinking and smoking are common among autistic people? Illegal drugs can become an issue for some autistic people. No doubt, vaping is common by now, too. Some say addictions and abusing substances are really about unresolved issues. Maybe they are. It's certainly true that autistic people have more of these than most because of our experiences.

I've mentioned before that suicide rates are higher within the autistic community than the general population. Researchers from Nottingham and Cambridge universities concluded that suicide levels among the autistic community are 'unacceptably high' – this doesn't surprise me at all. I might still be here, but I've thought about not being here many times. Who wouldn't? We're often treated like substandard human beings; unfit to exist alongside others for reasons we don't understand.

The trend towards suicide or suicidal thoughts is one that must be reversed. It shouldn't be hard to achieve, either, when kindness is all it takes. Everybody should be capable of that. Wilfully harming us because people believe we need to learn is neither okay nor helpful. It's never been appropriate.

So many issues, born from misunderstandings, contribute to the autistic reality. Autists are under-represented because so many don't have diagnoses. Instead, many are living half-lives under the strangulation of neurotypical expectation. There hasn't been a sudden explosion of autistic people, as some like to suggest, only an explosion in the number of people realising they may be on the spectrum and desperately needing answers. The waiting list for assessment by the NHS in the UK stands at around three years at the time of writing. Most people can see a doctor for a bunged-up nose faster than they'll get an ASD assessment.

While waiting, autists can watch their lives fall apart. They can lose their job and risk losing their home because they can't prove a recognised disability accounts for traits their

Eliza Jane Blake

employer perceives as not only undesirable, but unacceptable.

That's Dedication

There are many famous autistic people, but I won't name them. An internet trawl and celebrity biography search, however, will reveal some commonalities between them if it interests you. You'll find artists; actors; musicians and writers; scientists, mathematicians and tech specialists; not to mention a fair sprinkling of animal welfare champions and environmentalists.

Autistic people are passionate about their interests and we have the tenacity to see our projects through. We're often highly capable in our chosen field or in any job we undertake that appeals to us. The exceptions to this are those who face discouragement or negative projections from friends and family. We're as susceptible to negative judgements as anybody else.

Eliza Jane Blake

But most autists are highly creative, fair-minded, caring of others (including animals) and protective of nature. As I mentioned before, intelligence is a personal thing and not a factor in being autistic, but where intelligence is high, our analytical minds often excel in traditionally difficult subjects. Assessors of ASD look for enhanced pattern recognition skills as part of the assessment because they expect to find them and this trait plays a part in analytical thinking.

The detail-focus of our minds, when not dulled by depression or burnout, help artists to see clearly, musicians to hear the sounds they produce with precision and actors to immerse themselves in their characters. The scientists, mathematicians and technologists bring the same attention to their work because when we focus, the detail in any project can pop like we're seeing it through a magnifier. How ironic the over-stimulation of our brains that can cause problems in the workplace is also the reason for our increased productivity, precision and attention to detail.

Yes, some autists have learning difficulties and some will have exceptional intellectual ability. The spectrum of intellectual ability is as wide within the autistic community as it is in the neurotypical world. But the odds stack against us in the workplace because of our neurotype, regardless of intelligence and regardless of whether we have a diagnosis. This is despite our creative analytical approach to problem solving, reliability, focus and dedication to our work.

It's a shame employers value neurotypical social skills above other positives. Earlier in the book, I talked about how I object to the accusation of obsessive behaviour. I think that dedication is a much nicer word. It's a subtle shift, but one that turns a negative perception into a positive.

Smash The Boulder

Most neurotypicals don't realise the autists they assume to be stupid or naïve are often highly intelligent. Just because our brains work differently and process information from an opposing direction to neurotypicals, it doesn't make us idiots. I accept autists can be too trusting of others, or should that be, some neurotypicals are too quick to take advantage of others, but having processing delays doesn't automatically make us naïve and we're not stupid.

People used to assume that the physically disabled were incapable of working until they shouted (loudly) at a society blinded by ignorance, that their brains weren't lacking. Autistic people are in the same situation. Since receiving my diagnosis and declaring it, for the first time I've experienced being treated like a non-person. Other disabled people have complained about this for as long as I can remember, but now I know what they mean.

Having a neurodevelopmental disability doesn't mean that we're dense or backward. I accept I communicate and interpret the world around me differently and that I'm more capable than most in some ways, and less capable in others, but I'm not faulty. I still have a thinking brain and a voice, but even if I wasn't able to speak, as some autists can't, it wouldn't mean that my brain lacked intelligence. We're still human. Most of us can make our own decisions. We have a positive contribution to make.

Autistic people are usually honest, hardworking and reliable. Our attention-to-detail makes for employees with a record of conscientiousness and accuracy. Those autists who excel in niche industries, such as Information Technology, often achieve success despite their autistic brains. It's the rarity of their skills that employers value and which leads to any undesirable traits being ignored. Unfortunately, employers undervalue most average autists because of our differences in communication style and sociability. I hope that will change.

We know employers give more credit and value to employees who possess strong social skills, networking abilities, and the talent to shmooze, rather than to those who can fulfil their assigned roles in the most efficient way. Indeed, if an employee is socially popular, they're likely to keep their job even if they're not particularly good at it. This is a classic example of the neurotypical obsession, or dedication, to social skills and the excessively high credit they assign to anyone who displays them.

In truth, it's because autistic people are more focused on the job at hand than what was on TV last night that we're also often more productive than our neurotypical colleagues. A fact that counts for absolutely nothing – or so it would seem.

In our true contradictory style, though, we can be both the stickler and the rebel. We follow rules to the letter – literal interpretation – unless we think they're pointless, or a hindrance to efficiency, in which case we'll shamelessly ignore them. We accept, nurture and encourage those below us in rank, but can drive superiors to distraction by actively drawing attention to unnecessary inefficiencies because efficiency, productivity, and organisation matter to us.

Autists don't like obstructions, either physical or bureaucratic, and excel in devising efficient systems, monitoring performance indicators and finding solutions. It isn't true that all autists are good at maths, but many are drawn to careers that rely upon accuracy, predictability and exploration.

Smash The Boulder

Autists are usually creative. If we don't use our creativity at work, we'll most likely have creative hobbies and interests. But when given the opportunity, most of us would gladly bring creativity to our work. The most staid of autists may have the most imaginative flair if encouraged to open up.

How Hard can it Be?

So, autistic people, when allowed to thrive, can be the most productive, reliable, and hard-working people you could ever have on your team, but just like neurotypicals, we can't function properly when we're tiptoeing around on eggshells with our anxiety levels through the roof – not just because of sensory or information overload, but because we know we're being watched, monitored, criticised, held in contempt, blatantly treated unfairly compared to others and someone is often looking to get rid of us. When the problem is more about bruised egos than intentional offense, this is especially unfair.

Simple accommodations to manage our stress levels make a vast difference in our day-to-day existence and the neurotypical experience of working with us. Understanding why our differences exist and correcting the erroneous intent ascribed to them can make significant progress in improving our working relationships. Understanding can reduce the need for defensive mechanisms for all of us, allowing us to relax in each other's company. Unfortunately, autists often find our requests for accommodations at work denied, resented or considered unnecessary.

Reasonable adjustments can mean many things. For example, I mentioned before about the over-head strip lighting in offices giving me headaches. Just turning my desk so that I faced a window stopped the headaches. It was a simple, painless change that made a considerable difference to my physical well-being, but it didn't stop my co-workers begrudging me changing things.

At work, my colleagues often accused me of having an attitude problem and most of that was because of defensiveness resulting from all the accusations made against me that I didn't recognise. I've already acknowledged that we become defensive and hypervigilant because of this. But sometimes, there's a more sinister reason for our defensiveness. I'd like to relay to you what often happens to autistic people at work.

Please put yourself in our shoes for a second. Remember what I said about the struggles we can experience resulting from uncomfortable eye contact, literal interpretation (words and persona) the limited ability to read faces and body language, and then add processing delays to the mix. Unfortunately, there are many people who are, frankly, not gracious people when they believe they can get away with behaving badly.

The commonly held belief is that people are basically decent, but autistic people will probably dispute this assumption far more often than neurotypical people do because we're more likely to encounter people who aren't decent, or more accurately, we're more likely to be aware of who those people are because they seek us out. Unfortunately, once some people realise our limitations, they gleefully take advantage.

What they won't allow for, though, is that our limitations don't stem from a lack of intelligence. So, having seen our perceived shortcomings, they'll assume they can get away with just about anything and that we won't have a clue they're doing it. In us, they see entertainment on an otherwise humdrum day.

I've already introduced you to the traits of processing delays and pattern recognition. It's because of these two traits that those who lack integrity come unstuck. And this is how.

First, the not so nice person will realise a limitation exists. They will then test us to see how far they can push it and with each act or comment that they get away with, their confidence grows. Quickly, their natural arrogance will shine through when they're around us because they believe we're less than them; a muppet for them to play with who has no clue what they're doing.

At the same time this is happening, processing delays on our part may catch up and pattern recognition, kick in. There's no guarantee of what will or won't drop into our conscious thoughts later, but once we become aware, we'll make a mental note of each incident. It won't stop a similar situation from happening with this person and it won't mean that they won't be able to pull the same stunt on us again. It will, however, mean that when this or something similar has happened a few times, and it involves the same person, our pattern recognition skills will do their job and we'll know what we can expect from them. We may not draw attention to what we know, but from this moment on, we'll observe them.

The realisation in our minds of what they're doing usually occurs around the same time that their arrogance begins a gleeful dance before our eyes. Not surprisingly, this is when annoyance and anger begin on our part. If more than one person is involved in this offensive, mocking behaviour, we'll feel both hurt and furious. However, if we call them on it, their response will be denial. Always.

Autistic people know too well that some neurotypical people will lie with the ease of a swan gliding through calm waters. If we report the behaviour to management, they might speak to the person concerned, but will return with a shrug of the shoulder, saying they've denied it and that, therefore, there's nothing more they can do. In management's view, the matter is closed. Except, of course, it isn't.

This is where we need decent neurotypicals to put themselves in our shoes. If they had the limitations that we live with, and they knew that someone in their midst was prepared to take advantage of those limitations, would they want that person, or persons, anywhere near them, or would they want to protect themselves – particularly if it's clear nothing is going to be done to stop them because there's no proof; it's our word against theirs, and the person concerned is happy to lie about it?

We know what we can expect from that person. We know we're vulnerable to their behaviour. With or without a diagnosis, we know that awareness of that person won't be enough to protect us as it would for most people. This is, in part, why society recognises us as disabled. It's a way in which we're vulnerable. We also know that everyone else thinks the sun shines out of that person's posterior, because their behaviour around those who would see straight through them is very different to how they behave in front of us.

Not only are we alone in our experience, as we often are, now we're standing alone while everyone else sides with the disingenuous one because they can't relate to our experience of that person and believe them to be decent.

Management and everyone else will now start accusing us of being the problem. We're being hostile. We're being rude. Obviously, we've misunderstood that person. Meanwhile, the real 'problem' will put on a good show in front of everybody else. They'll be upset by our hurtful accusations. We've misinterpreted their words or actions and they can't possibly imagine what they've done to deserve our attitude. On top of their original behaviour, they've now gone all out to convince everyone else, including management, that it's all in our heads. There's a term for this now. It's called gaslighting, and it happens to autistic people a lot.

Were we imagining their behaviour? Of course not. If we were, the person concerned would try to convince us of how we misunderstood them. They wouldn't be throwing blatant smug smirks in our direction when nobody else is watching.

It's in situations like this where it's right to recognise the autistic brain as a disability. The neurotypical advice to be more aware, as they would be, is pointless. The limitations are a fact of our neurotype. Our brains will always instinctively take words literally and others at face value. There will always be limits to what we can read in a person's face and we'll always have processing delays – even if we know what someone is like, we may not realise the significance of what they've said or done until it's too late. The concentration and hypervigilance it takes for us to beat our inherent brain function can cause burnout in no time at all.

So, for these reasons, most of us don't want that person anywhere near us. Once they've shown us how low they're prepared to sink and how willing they are to take advantage of our limitations, we can't afford to let that person be in our orbit, and knowing what we can expect from them and what they're capable of, doesn't change that.

The alternative is a simmering anger every time we realise they've done it to us again, and eventually, there'll be an explosion on our part for which we can expect further punishment from those who don't recognise our predicament. Maybe if we never realised what those people were doing, it wouldn't harm us so much, but we do. It's just a delayed recognition.

Autistic people are usually inherently honest. This isn't only clear in the way we verbally communicate; it also applies to how we are with people: our persona. We can't pretend to get on with someone when we know we can't trust them. If we do, it won't be long before we've put the prior incidents behind us and we're once again vulnerable to their behaviour. Unfortunately, in situations like this, the generous nature of autistic people works against us.

It's also true that once burned, we'll become hypervigilant about protecting ourselves. What else can we do? We can't change the behaviour of people who lack integrity and we can't change the way our brains function. If we don't distance ourselves from people we can't trust, those lacking integrity are free to bide their time and repeat their actions when we're not paying attention, and as a result, both they and everyone else will label us idiots. So, we're caught between a rock and a hard place. No matter what we do, we lose.

Unless other people recognise there's a reason we do what we do and start listening to us when we say we can't trust someone. It's not the keeping of one person at a distance that's the problem for us, it's how that person will then manipulate everyone around them to pick a side and condemn us for having the audacity to stand up to them. Instead of only needing to keep one person at arm's length, we stand accused of treating a saint badly and end up isolated by pack rule. The speed most others are prepared to be manipulated by these people is mind-blowing and the arrogant manipulator is always so proud of their cleverness.

It's this social element, the need to hold the pack together, that isolates us further. Unfortunately, management's need for us to accept what has happened and move on ignores the risk it exposes us to. We know we're vulnerable to the manipulations of some people and we recognise the need to protect ourselves from them. Insisting we mingle with these people, like the issue never happened, rather than keep our distance, raises our stress levels and increases the need for hypervigilance that will ultimately negatively affect our mental and physical health. Please don't ask or expect us to compromise our well-being in this way. It's the only protection we have.

Unfortunately, it's also because of these negative experiences we may misinterpret someone who genuinely means no harm. If we're approached by a neurotypical who wants to help resolve a situation, but who does it in a neurotypical way, i.e., they don't ask a direct question and try to lead us into revealing what we're thinking instead, the feeling of being manipulated is the same. It still feels underhand.

It's because of this that autists don't like and find the neurotypical way of communicating offensive. Our brains aren't wired to seek subtext. The indirect way of encouraging others to open up and volunteer information, rather than asking for it, always feels underhand; particularly when neurotypicals use it against us to manipulate us into revealing information when they have an ulterior motive for wanting it or they're being intrusive and have no right to ask.

Another thing we find hard to stomach is the neurotypical belief that it's okay to fake friendliness when management has ordered them to put any disagreements aside or because they want to manipulate us into revealing something personal. Besides being disingenuous, this is behaviour we find confusing.

Consider what I've already covered about literal interpretation and problems reading faces and body language. When people smile at us and talk in a friendly manner, we take them on face value and assume them to be genuine. Regardless of whether the intention is to mislead or to move on from a prior incident because they're expected to by management; we're being conned. Knowing people do this because it's expected of the neurotypical style doesn't help us. We're open and trusting by nature and people who lack integrity use this against us. Sadly, it's because of our awareness of those people and the vulnerability it causes that we find fake friendliness so offensive, even when there's no dishonest intent.

As with our need for direct communication, we need honest interactions. It won't bother us if people choose to give us a wide berth, we'd rather know where we stand, but please don't mislead or confuse us with fake friendliness. Or worse, do so because making fun of us in this way is entertaining.

The construction of the social world heavily favours neurotypicals. By design, it suits their commonly occurring brain function and leaves little scope for compromise to help those who struggle in the neurotypical world. But often, perceived autistic attitude problems have neurotypical manipulative behaviour, or spiteful vindictiveness born from a desire to punish us, at its root.

Accommodations at work aren't a demand for preferential treatment. They acknowledge the ways in which our brains work differently, recognise that our needs are not the same, and allow us to be comfortable and protected within our environment. This comfort reduces the likelihood of overwhelm striking with consequences for everybody.

The negative consequences associated with autistic brains don't occur in controlled and considerate environments. Awareness and compassion are all it takes. There's no need for us to be side-lined or banished to the fringes of society. We're only asking to be treated with the respect and kindness neurotypicals expect for themselves, rather than unrelenting shameless hostility.

Condemnation, bullying and the silent treatment aren't appropriate responses to autistic traits, but without education within the workplace, this is what happens. The knowledge of why those differences exist, and how to respond helpfully, would go a long way to reducing the judgements, bullying and vilification of autistic people in the workplace. If the majority

Smash The Boulder

recognised that how others think and communicate isn't about them, we'd all get along much better.

The Autistic Reality

The neurotypical world recognises having an autistic brain as having a neurodevelopmental disorder. As someone with the intelligence to write a book, I find this assessment quite arrogant. It is, however, true that our maturity as young adults can be slower than our peers.

It's also true that despite not having intellectual disabilities, I'm still child-like at heart. Even now, I wouldn't be able to resist a bouncy castle at a party in a private garden. I still allow myself to enjoy those aspects of life that appeal to me with a child-like exuberance. When I take off my mask, and nowadays I try to keep the mask off as often as I'm able, I'm still very much in touch with my inner child and I don't want to lose that. I object to being expected to hide it.

I remember as a thirteen-year-old coming home from my grandparents to find my mother had decorated my bedroom in pink. I hate pink, or at least I did then. It's just about tolerable now. The point is, my mother knew I'd hate it, but did it anyway. She believed I needed to stop being a tomboy and start behaving like a girl. Her decision was entirely age related and skewed by societal expectations.

She also bought a duvet for my bed. They were very expensive at the time and my mother never spent money that she didn't have to. She did it because, in her opinion, I needed to learn how to get in and out of bed properly. I mentioned before how I would slide in and out of bed without un-tucking my bed sheets. At thirteen, she thought I should've grown out of this. I hated that duvet. I hated how lightweight it was and how loosely it rested on me. Even wrapping it around and under me didn't restore the feeling of sleeping under tight blankets.

The expectation to be neurotypical was a big thing that started young. Society's inability to accept difference as normal negatively affected anyone who didn't meet those inflexible tick-box rules. We've come a long way. When I was at school, they didn't allow girls to wear trousers unless there was six inches of snow on the ground. When I began my first job, management wouldn't allow me to wear trousers. I had to wear a skirt.

The push to recognise diversity and encourage inclusion has made a difference for many people at work, but not for autistic workers, because society still sees our difference as a behavioural issue rather than a difference in brain chemistry. Until society recognises differences in brain function as normal, people with the ability to contribute to society will continue to be side-lined.

Eliza Jane Blake

So, the only option for autistic workers is to fake it. For me, this is extremely difficult because I'm not very good at it and I'm not alone in this struggle. My inherent honesty struggles with the expectation I should pretend to be someone I'm not and my ability to wear a mask varies from day to day depending on the stresses I face. But regardless, as a young adult, the fake me became the adult me and the pressure of uncomfortable expectation has much to answer for.

Without exception, people accept the fake me as the real me, but it's flawed, and in some respects, causes me more problems. No matter how able I am to hold an adult conversation and even speak with uncompromising authority sometimes, I'm prone to processing delays. I often can't find the word I want at the right time during verbal exchanges and in my haste to speak words before I forget them, they often tumble over each other. Not surprisingly, I prefer to communicate in writing, not only for the reasons I've just stated, but because it gives me a chance to measure my response and ensure I haven't been too direct or abrupt. It also grants me time to consider the other person's words, too. It buys me time to see things I would otherwise miss.

People know some autists can have phenomenal memories, but memory issues are common for autistic people. While those with excellent memories have a brain that functions like a highly organised and efficient computer, I liken mine to an underground cave with a hole at ground level. New information pours through the hole and lands on top of whatever is already there, over and over. The obvious problem is that when I want to retrieve something, I can't find it. It's a common problem that can make me seem like I don't have a clue what I'm talking about when the knowledge is there... it's just hiding... with a big smirk on its face.

None of which should deter a business from employing autistic people. Most autists with memory issues have exceptional organisational abilities because we know that if we haven't written something down, the memory may well disappear in a puff of smoke, like it never existed.

The worst thing about a lifetime of masking is that there comes a point when autistic people can lose sight of who they really are. It doesn't happen to everybody, but years of masking autistic traits and trying not to upset those around us results in very real consequences. The more severely an autist's family demonstrated their displeasure with them, the more likely the autist is to hold the view they mustn't bow to their autistic traits and will seek to bury them.

I've pointed out previously that living a lie every day directly causes depression, which is a very real and debilitating condition. Every time we step outside the front door, even when we're at home if we live with neurotypicals, we wear that mask. How can this not be exhausting?

The refusal of society to allow us to be who we really are has a massive impact on our mental health and wellbeing. Everybody wants to be accepted, but we shouldn't have to deny or compromise who we are to achieve that. Rejecting and side-lining people as a punishment for not conforming to the unwritten neurotypical standards is harsh, inflexible and shouldn't be happening. I'm tired of being punished for being different and not being able to think in the same way as most people. My brain isn't faulty. In some respects, it works exceptionally well, but it does work differently.

Eliza Jane Blake

It also spent the past eight years struggling to function at all because of a combination of burnout, depression and the consequence of other medical conditions that slowed my brain to the point of being so sluggish, it wasn't working properly. I don't want to keep fighting against a boulder of erroneous beliefs that stubbornly refuse to compromise. I hope, this book will help raise awareness and encourage progress, but for now, the only way I can protect my brain is by working from home as often as I'm able and limiting my exposure to this chaotic world as far as I reasonably can. Many other autistic people are doing the same thing, but we shouldn't have to.

If there's one thing that's really stood out for me while researching the autistic reality over the past few years, it's how many employers put autistic people into measures at work or dismiss them from their jobs because of an intolerance of autistic traits.

No other minority group finds themselves subjected to such blatant discrimination in the workplace. Not anymore. It's not acceptable to discriminate against a black person, a gay person, a person of different ethnic or religious origin, and it's not acceptable to discriminate against autistic people, but how can we uphold this when managers don't know what autistic brain function looks like and company policies support disciplinary procedures against common autistic traits?

Even if an autistic person declares their neurotype as a disability, it means nothing. The ignorance about what being autistic entails and how it may present is absolute, unless someone with authority within an organisation has first-hand knowledge of what it can look like and that doesn't happen very often.

Smash The Boulder

In a previous chapter I pointed out how neurotypicals would feel if the constant hail of criticism that's levelled at us fell to them instead: the confusion they would experience, the hurt they would feel and the fear that would take hold, either on a conscious or unconscious level, swirling around in their heads resulting in paranoia that they might inadvertently say the wrong thing. This is the autistic reality in the workplace and is the reason we walk around on eggshells in this neurotypical world. It's at the root of the nervousness we experience in the presence of other people and our well-known awkwardness.

It's true, our different communication styles aren't compatible, but they are what they are. Autistic people don't deserve to be wiped off the planet just because people don't like the way our brains work. The status quo is extremely one-sided and self-serving. We're all human beings and either we all matter or nobody matters.

We know neurotypicals place an exceptionally high value on soft skills and socialising, just as we place a high value on productivity and accuracy, but is a difference in priorities really a reason to get rid of someone, particularly when the one being rejected is the one whose priority is doing a good job? This is the absurdity I and many other autists struggle to get our heads around, but it also highlights the uphill battle we face for equality.

Cancel culture is unhelpful, to say the least, but many people haven't acknowledged this yet. There are always two sides to every story and all that's required is a willingness from both sides to understand and work with the other. We can achieve this, and I desperately want to see change and the rise of autistic rights. But I want to achieve this through mutual respect, not accusations and uncompromising nastiness.

There are autistic people who also favour cancel culture, although I think this is a direct reaction to the treatment we receive in society, and I understand the anger. We have a right to be angry and a right to be heard. But screaming at people doesn't encourage anyone to listen any more than mumbling into the back of a hand.

I don't doubt I'll receive hostile judgement for writing this book, not only from those neurotypicals who prefer to believe the autistic brain doesn't exist, but from within the autistic community itself. It's sad, but unfortunately, we don't all see the world through the same eyes. Regardless, I'll have my say in spite of who may not like it.

Workplace culture needs to change by integrating different strengths and skills and embracing different neurotypes. We all have something to contribute. We need the neurotypical community to allow neurodiversity to exist in the workplace, because presently, it doesn't. People like to think it does, but they only really allow it from within the confines of their own experience and expectations. Expansion of the mind must happen before autists can relax within the society that we're also a part of.

We live on the fringes, pushed to the side so that we don't upset the sensitivities of the majority. We don't want to tiptoe around, constantly in a state of anxiety because we're afraid of upsetting someone and being punished for it. I know my anxiety issues only developed after repeated hammerings from people who were intolerant of my traits. As a young child, I was happy to be myself. The photos of me as a child show a grinning, mischievous imp with trouble written all over her. I was happy. I was authentic. I was even relaxed when talking to others, but all that stopped because, as I grew older, tolerance withdrew. Expectations to recognise and understand the neurotypical way of being, and to change my communication style, became more insistent. I quickly learned that people disapproved of most things I said or did. But I couldn't force my instinctive brain function to work differently.

So, the mocking belittlements started. The blatant condescension kicked in. I soon fought back. Not physically, but by throwing mocking belittlements and criticism back at others. Completely understandable because those who were so quick to judge and condemn me were far from perfect themselves. But then the criticism about being critical of others began. It seems those who were so quick to criticise how I came across weren't so keen on having their own shortcomings pointed out to them. However, when attacked on a personal level, and that was how the criticisms came across, why wouldn't I return fire?

We talk in different languages. That's all. But is that a reason for autistic people to be wiped out? That's what many neurotypicals want to do to us even if they don't realise it. So many need everyone to be just like they are because that convinces them they're okay; that it's not them who's getting it wrong. This treadmill needs to stop.

We don't all have to be the same. It isn't okay to make anybody's life a fraught nightmare, but that's how many autistic people feel. Society subjects autistic people to uncompromising demands to change in a way designed to meet their own needs at our expense, and in the workplace, management often upholds those demands.

Eliza Jane Blake

Constantly criticising people does a lot of harm. The source of the criticism for us isn't only our peers, but teachers and caregivers during childhood. Where families are concerned, there's often no end to it. This constant stream of punishments, inflicted often for things we can't control or don't understand within ourselves, destroys our self-esteem, confidence, and ability to live a fulfilling life. This is then something else society will punish us for: our failure to succeed, according to the neurotypical definition of what success is. Unless we have skills that most others lack, for example, advanced IT skills, we find ourselves pushed aside and under-employed until we have nowhere left to go, no faith in our own abilities and no motivation to try any more.

We need the neurotypical community to take a massive step back and remove their egos from the equation. Yes, I said that out loud. Much of the cycle of contempt and punishment we face has bruised or fragile egos at its heart.

Maybe a flash of venting happened or an autistic person has said something that somebody doesn't like. Maybe the autist isn't friendly enough. Or maybe their efforts to fit in simply aren't hitting the mark. Removing autistic people from their employment so that neurotypicals don't have to stretch their comfort zones is a poor way to behave, but many people, particularly the neurotic and uncompromising, think this is acceptable. It's a reflection of how only some bruised egos matter, but we, too, have egos.

The assertion of people in the past who believed that autistic traits reflected poor behaviour or rudeness, has served the neurotypical monopoly over the world of work, well. But it can't continue. Racist. Homophobic. Ageist. Sexist. What's the word? There isn't one for those who discriminate

Smash The Boulder

against those who're autistic, but I'm sure there should be. Our difference being a disability doesn't give anybody the right to assume that we shouldn't be able, or allowed, to work alongside others. The physically disabled won that argument a long time ago.

There's no excuse for places of work being school playgrounds for its daily inhabitants. Some managers will stamp out the bullying of unpopular employees, but all too often, the managers are the worst culprits and think nothing of abusing their position as managers to get rid of perfectly able employees so that they don't have to work with them.

'You're not in my gang!' This attitude annoys me more than any other simply because it still exists. Many autists get bullied at school. Many find themselves picked on relentlessly, and the one thing that keeps them going is the knowledge that school isn't forever; that they won't be stuck with these people every day once school is done, because they'll be living in the world of adults. Ahem...

Adults may prefer to call their gangs cliques, but they boil down to the same thing: we don't like you and we won't pretend to tolerate you. Go away. Too often, the fact they haven't realised the world doesn't spin for their sole benefit doesn't stop them from getting their own way.

Take a moment to think about that. Once assessed and diagnosed with ASD, doctors automatically recognise us as neurologically disabled and yet the full burden of the responsibility for understanding others, and bending to fit in, rests on us. How can that ever be reasonable? Now consider that there are so many undiagnosed autists, particularly among the older population. They don't even know there's been a concrete reason for their struggles, but still face relentless punishment, assuming they haven't already retreated from public life or from living altogether.

Some autists think it's unnecessary or inappropriate that we're all classed as disabled. I take their point, but as always, it's not that simple.

Level it Up

Some countries assign a category to autistic people. There are three levels, with 1 being the least and 3 being the most. Sounds confusing? That's because the levels denote support needs, but people often miss this important distinction, resulting in confusion and a misinterpretation that the levels imply affectedness such as mild or severe, or that some of us are more autistic than others. As I've already explained, we're all equally autistic. There's no such thing as being 'a bit autistic'. It's the level of support we need that varies.

The countries who adopt the levels system do so for their own benefit, i.e., the three levels are a construct created by the system, for the system. They're a marker that denotes a person's need for support. As I mentioned before, nobody receives a diagnosis without having traits that significantly affect their life and the misinterpretation of the levels system results in level 1 autists being assumed to need no help. The assumption that we don't struggle is incredibly damaging.

Level 1 autists are no less susceptible to autistic ventings and shutdowns, to literal interpretation, to misunderstandings in communication, to processing delays, to relationship problems across the board (family, friends, colleagues and partners) to hyper-focus, to a lack of self-awareness – often because we're focussed on something else – to paranoia because of the volume of misunderstandings with others, to problems shifting gears, to depression because of the misunderstandings and subsequent punishments as our managers discipline our perceived faults.

It's a combination of the misinterpretation of the levels system, misunderstandings about our traits, and the high level of ignorance that surrounds the reality of autistic brain function that leaves many of us feeling abandoned or written off. Even before I knew my diagnosis or had any inkling that my brain chemistry differed from other people, I felt like I'd lived my life with one arm tied behind my back. I just didn't know why.

No matter what I did or how hard I tried, my efforts were never enough. Knowing the truth now doesn't help me in the world of work. I can't switch off my autistic brain now any more than I could when I was younger and my CV simply doesn't reflect my abilities because society has never allowed me to get on in a world that prioritises neurotypical soft skills over ability and productivity. Worse than that, society continues to run autists out of the workplace while claiming to be inclusive.

Smash The Boulder

When I finally received my diagnosis, and with it the understanding that explained my life experience, it sounded ridiculous that anyone could have a debilitating neuro-disability for such a long time without knowing. But I'm far from alone. How it happened is shockingly simple. First, autistic people accept their brain function and thought processes just as neurotypical people accept theirs. For each, it's normal and we don't question it. Second, just like neurotypical people, autists also face brainwashing on a massive scale to know that autistic traits are undesirable and unacceptable. Being unable to defy them just makes us feel worse.

My experience is far from unique to my generation. Our carers, teachers and peers made it clear our struggles were of our own making. The assumption was always that we weren't trying hard enough, that we should know better by now, or that we were just rude or disrespectful. Our thought processes and communication style were a choice to be condemned. The inability to control our emotions was clearly a personality defect to be stamped out and our sensory issues a shameless demonstration of melodramatic, irrational behaviour to be ridiculed out of us.

Those who could see the difference in us never questioned why our struggles existed or considered there could be something else behind it. Schools were only interested if a child was being disruptive or falling behind, and all too often, our parents were more concerned about stigma than asking the right questions. Unlike the younger generation today, most of us had no access to support services; we had to find our own way to survive in a hostile world – with mixed results. Unfortunately, in some ways, little has changed. In the workplace, managers and coworkers still hold intelligent autists to a standard that's incompatible with our brain function and punish us relentlessly when we don't meet neurotypical expectations.

At present, even though society designates autistic people under the disabled umbrella, it doesn't stop discrimination in the workplace because most people have an unrealistic and outdated view of what autistic people look like and of our capabilities. It's level 1 autists who're most likely trying to exist in the workplace and having doors slammed in their faces when they can't meet the expectations of their neurotypical peers and bosses. But this is going to change.

I'm confident society will recognise autistic brains as an alternative neurotype, but to understand why, we need to consider the history that's led us to where we are now.

Experts recognised 'autism' as a condition as far back as the early 1900s, and over time, its definition changed as research progressed. Initially, researchers assumed it to be some kind of childhood schizophrenia and, later, a mental handicap. On this basis, many autistic children found themselves taken from their families and placed in institutions. During the time before any sort of welfare system came into existence, this was the norm.

As an autistic person, I can't think of anything more frightening than being taken away from my parents and put into a noisy environment with strangers who had no incentive to care and where I can imagine the regime to be inflexible and harmful to autistic people, particularly if they couldn't communicate verbally or had extreme sensory issues. Our regular hospitals at the time were strict about how they expected patients to behave. If the authority figures in the institutions were as rigid as Matron, I can't imagine it would have been an easy ride for any autistic resident.

The provision of state-run institutions may have helped families who needed to work for financial survival in the absence of a welfare state, but it may also be responsible for the reluctance of parents to acknowledge any kind of problem with their child's development for fear of the state taking their child away from them. This fear could be at the root of the stigma that prevented many autists of my generation, give or take a few years, from receiving the help they needed as children. It's likely people passed down the imperative need for denial through the generations as a gut reaction, even if they didn't explicitly state why.

This situation continued for many years with no tangible progress made in understanding the breadth of autistic traits or the extent of occurrence in the population until the closure of the institutions between the 1960s and 1980s. Until this time, researchers had only studied those with the highest support needs. They hadn't known that those with obvious disabilities shared traits with other children who didn't display any intellectual disability. This situation is probably responsible for the persistent incorrect belief that all autistic people have learning disabilities. It wasn't until those children capable of integrating into mainstream schools began mixing with other children that researchers noticed the similarities.

In 1980, the DSM-3 (The Statistical Manual of Mental Disorders 3rd edition, published by the American Psychiatric Association [APA]) listed autism as a separate diagnosis, rather than a kind of schizophrenia. That was only forty-four years ago. In 1994, the DSM-4 recognised several diagnoses under the autism umbrella. The DSM-5 progressed to

Eliza Jane Blake

recognising the autistic spectrum as one diagnosis when the APA published again in 2013, and when the ICD11 (The International Classification of Diseases 11th edition – used in the UK) published a few years later, it agreed with the DSM-5 albeit, minus a levels system, while acknowledging a distinction between autists with or without intellectual disability. It was the DSM-5 that created the diagnosis of Autistic Spectrum Disorder and at the time of writing; this was only eleven years ago.

Each progression in the research has been a positive step for autistic people, although many believe it doesn't go far enough. However, considering how recently the APA recognised the extent of difference within the autistic community and made this addition to the manual, many of us hope the recognition of the autistic brain as a neurotype won't be far behind. After all, the spectrum recognises that we all have identifiable common traits, just as neurotypicals do. We also have varying levels of intelligence, just as neurotypicals do, and we have individual personalities and interests, just as neurotypicals do. So, we're all different while sharing common traits. How is that not a neurotype? The only 'benefit' of calling our type a disorder is that the majority neurotype can claim a rightness over our wrongness, and without conscience, treat us as irrelevant because we're recognised as neurologically disabled.

Incidentally, if you noticed I've mostly avoided using the term 'autism' throughout this book, it's partly because it makes us sound like we have a disease when we don't, and mainly because I've never heard the majority neurotype acknowledged as neurotypicalism. (The software I'm using to write this has just flagged up my use of a non-existent word in bright red.) When we restore balance and embrace equality, I'll consider jumping off my high-horse on this one. But not before.

Some autistic people believe the disabled or disordered label doesn't reflect who they are. Others consider it to be part of their identity. For me, finally receiving an answer that confirmed I wasn't mad or imagining things was a relief, but I objected to suddenly becoming labelled disabled after receiving so many years of contempt and I still don't accept the term 'disorder' as I find it incredibly arrogant. The 1990s Concise Oxford Dictionary defines a disorder as: 1 a lack of order, 2 a riot; a commotion, 3 Med. A usually minor ailment or disease.

I'm not mentally defective. My brain doesn't have either a minor ailment or a disease. Indeed, my brain performs exceptionally well in most regards, most of the time. I hate having to acknowledge that the autistic difference is also a disability, but unfortunately, it needs to be this way, at least for now. It's true that unscrupulous people in our society manipulate and take advantage of autistic people, so I accept I am disabled in this world simply because I will always be vulnerable to those people who lack integrity and the disabled label is the only protection I, and every other autistic person, has against those who abuse or discredit us in the workplace. But disordered? No.

As smart as I can be in some ways, I can't change my brain chemistry, and more importantly, I don't want to. Without my passion (neurotypical interpretation: obsession) with books and the written word, I wouldn't be writing this now; trying to improve my community's relationship with the majority neurotype. Instead, I'd be trying to fit in by nursing a drink at the pub, while pickling my liver and chain-smoking to give my hands something to do. It's truly liberating to not feel compelled to do that anymore, but there again, I found it easier to talk rubbish when I was drunk, and for a few hours, probably did actually fit in, while genuinely not caring what anybody thought of me. Maybe that was a release in itself, albeit an unhealthy one.

The classification of all autistic individuals as disabled is a topic that can be argued in the future. Right now, I don't see how we can't be without becoming more vulnerable, but who knows, with tolerance and acceptance, maybe it won't be necessary. But for now, all autistic people are effectively aliens trying to exist in a foreign land just because our brains' software is in a minority.

Regardless of where some may assume a person lies in the spectrum, an autist may or may not have intellectual disabilities, but will still be susceptible to both ventings (or meltdowns if they prefer) and shutdowns, sensory issues, processing delays and a myriad of problems associated with social communication that cause us to be ostracised by an unforgiving society. Now raise your hands if this paragraph proves our disability. Maybe it does, or maybe the world should consider my words in the context that these traits only present themselves, or are an issue, *because* we live in a neurotypical world.

If our needs had priority, we would eliminate the triggers that cause us these social problems without a second thought. But they don't. We live in a world dominated by neurotypicals; designed by them and for them.

Neurotypicals would struggle to exist in our ideal world. The quiet. The lack of crowds. Dimmed lighting. No uniforms.

Smash The Boulder

Comfort and practicality before aesthetics (unless fashion is of particular interest). No pointless rules. A level field based on mutual respect for our individual strengths rather than a rigid hierarchy built on the mastery of neurotypical social skills. Lively and passionate debates between like-minded people, but no small talk. Problems addressed and resolved completely rather than 'bodged' with temporary sticking-plaster solutions. Relationships where each person cares about the other, but spends most of their time doing what interests them, rather than being chained together at every opportunity – unless they share the same interests.

It would be a very different world and I don't doubt neurotypicals would find it lonely and isolating. The communication style their brains instinctively adopt would meet with frowns and scowls for being unclear. People would discourage their presumptuous nature. They would feel like their needs didn't matter. Their inherent aversion to voicing potentially painful truths would land them in trouble regularly, and their manipulative natures would probably see them in prison.

In this context, we can only perceive disability as subjective. The side of the fence any of us stands on will dictate our impression of which is right or wrong, unless we agree there is no right or wrong. In time, I hope autists won't need the protection of disabled status unless they can't live independently. I'd like us all to recognise what the differences are and why they exist so that we can all be ourselves without offending each other or fearing unnecessary and inappropriate retribution.

As you now know, The Spectrum isn't linear, and it isn't possible to take a list of symptoms and decide where any

Eliza Jane Blake

autist lies on the spectrum. Our traits will affect us in different ways, not just as regular variations, but on different days, depending on what is happening in our lives and our exposure to various triggers. Yes, some autists are non-speaking, but speaking autists can become non-speaking in some situations and neither reality reflects intelligence or a lack of it. Sometimes, whether we can speak is a consequence of exposure to stimuli or triggers, but mostly, how we communicate is a default setting in our brain. Just as the neurotypical brain has its default setting, so does ours. The wiring of neurotypical brains is no more a conscious choice than how the wiring in an autistic brain works.

Being autistic isn't a choice. Ventings and shutdowns aren't a choice. Processing delays aren't a choice. Problems with sensory stimuli aren't a choice. Literal interpretation isn't a choice. Direct communication isn't a choice. Denial of our communication style can be a choice, but not all of us can do that, and many who can, pay the price at a later time. Our differences are a consequence of different brain chemistry, not behavioural problems, and our ability to meet the daily challenges autists face is a variable, not a constant. Just as neurotypicals have days when everything that can go wrong, does. Some days, everything that can trigger us finds a way into our orbit.

People don't like change, I know that, and the change I'm advocating is big. It's huge, in fact. And reversing an urge to stamp out autistic traits and embrace us instead takes effort. Taking a step back from bruised egos and pride will be hard for some, but not impossible. Not if people remember that it's highly unlikely we intend to cause offense. The turnaround in thinking is a massive reversal and the roots of ingrained beliefs are strong, stubbornly so, but this change must happen.

Those who advocate for the cure of autistic people should ask themselves if they find it acceptable to expect black people to have a bath in bleach, or if they think it's acceptable to expect gay people to undergo aversion therapy. Being autistic isn't a disease, it's merely a particular style of brain function. One woman I interacted with on the internet displayed hostility towards autistic people on a level that seemed like she believed extermination was a reasonable solution. Her attitude was absolutely shocking, but she's not alone in her belief that society shouldn't allow autistic people to breathe the same air as them.

Autistic people want to live their lives without fear of prejudice and persecution in the workplace. Many believe my dream is just wishful thinking, but Margaret Thatcher never thought she'd see a female Prime Minister in her lifetime, so here's hoping.

There needs to be a recognition that there is more than one neurotype rather than society clinging to the belief that anyone who differs from the majority has a disorder or is less is some way. We now know that autistic brain function doesn't mean severely disabled. Many autistic people have brains that are intelligent, willingly contribute to society, and can live independently. Many others want to do the same, but find the doors locked and bolted. Some have made significant contributions to society. There's no justification for the oppression we face, beyond making neurotypical lives easier, and that's not okay.

There is more than one way to be and more than one way to think, but standards in the workplace are currently rigidly neurotypical and make no allowance for difference. So certain are neurotypicals of their rightness, the arrogance of the situation doesn't seem to register. For many, assigning a person a label and getting rid of any 'problem' people is the simple solution.

Attitudes need to change. The language needs to change. Beliefs need to change and together we can do that.

All Aboard

So, until now I've mainly spoken about neurotypicals in a general sense and not addressed you, the reader, directly. This is where I change that. I hope I've explained the differences between us clearly without causing too much offense or generating too much resistance.

This chapter is a summary of ways that may help us work alongside each other. It may sound like it's a one-way street with me asking neurotypicals to make all the effort, and in some ways, it is, but please remember that autistic people are already aware of most neurotypical expectations even if we can't meet them. We've been told how we should be, our whole lives, so, I'm not saying that we don't have any effort to make, I'm just asking that neurotypicals attempt to meet us halfway. I'll start with some general requests that don't assume all autists have a diagnosis and then move on to more specific things.

The first thing I'd ask is to keep an open mind. Think about how any initial assumption may not be accurate. Consider if the person displays autistic traits before making a judgement.

Try not to judge those who struggle with small talk – if they're autistic, it won't be a personal rejection. We just find this sort of conversation excruciatingly difficult. Instead, find out what our interests are and encourage us to talk about them – just be aware, we may not know when to stop and might end up boring you if we think you're actually interested!

Sorry about that, but you can just say, 'whoa! Too much information—' and most autists would be unlikely to take offense at such a direct statement. Disappointed, possibly, that we haven't got the willing audience we thought we had, but that's not the same thing. We might even laugh at our mistake if we feel comfortable rather than judged.

Allow people to be quiet without judgement when that's who they are. Autists can be noisy sometimes, but we're also likely to be quiet and probably don't even realise we're doing it – our brains are so active we're hearing conversations in our heads all the time, so we don't notice external quiet like neurotypicals do. This is also not a personal rejection.

If someone seems to be a nice and friendly person, but then explodes unexpectedly, please know that your initial assessment was probably accurate. Refrain from making harsh judgements or assuming the person needs to be taught how to behave or face exclusion until they learn. Just walk away. If it's possible to remove the source of the upset, do so. In the meantime, make some discreet observations and check for any other signs of autistic traits.

Smash The Boulder

Train staff to walk away from any potential instance of autistic venting or meltdown and, under no circumstances, should anybody confront or challenge someone who is venting. If that person is autistic, they're experiencing very high stress levels, and any attempt to intervene can make the situation a lot worse, either by sending them into a shutdown or by extending the duration of the episode.

We know how hard venting episodes can be for everyone and that the autistic person feels a lot worse than the observers do afterwards. We don't want to be having them any more than you want to be witnessing them. Train staff to understand that some people don't have the same ability to handle stress as others and that this isn't a reflection of character or personality. Stepping back from ego-driven expectations of punishment and remembering that kindness and empathy go a long way to healing a situation faster than recrimination, will benefit everyone involved. Work with us to identify triggers and produce a plan to prevent them from happening in the future, but please note that it may take us longer to verbalise what happened than it would you, so approach it gently and without contempt.

If we've said no to something when you wanted a yes, don't hound us to change our response to the one that you wanted to hear. If we could meet the request, we wouldn't have said no anyway, and continuing to push us will increase stress levels, leading to a potential venting episode. The same applies to encouraging us to work harder. Autists rarely need these prompts.

Avoid giving the 'rubbish' tasks to someone who is socially unpopular – it breeds a sense of injustice and most autistic people already feel misunderstood, unappreciated, judged, gossiped about and accused of things they don't recognise to be true.

Ask about any sensory issues we have and discuss how the impact of those issues can be mitigated. (This is usually more easily achieved than most would imagine.)

Avoid making loud or sudden noises. Avoid shouting in a quiet environment. Be aware of how bright the lighting is and how hot the working temperature is. Are there any powerful smells that might have a detrimental effect?

Staring intently to force eye contact creates discomfort, and sometimes even pain, for autists. Be considerate and aware that things that don't affect neurotypicals may well have a negative effect on autists.

Be direct. I haven't met an autist yet who would not rather people be direct and blunt than drop hints that we either miss altogether or which just confuse us.

Avoid dragging us out of hyper-focus. When our concentration is so complete that we're unaware of our surroundings, hauling us back up to civilisation, unexpectedly, is a shock to the system on a par with being woken from a deep sleep and can elicit a similar reaction, i.e., you may need to jump back and can probably expect some immediate irritation!

You might also speak to us and assume that we're ignoring you when a response isn't forthcoming. We're not ignoring you. This is how intense hyper-focus can be. We drop into this state without realising it's happening and aren't aware of everything in the background falling away from our consciousness. It may be disconcerting if it's not realised that we really haven't heard you, but it's also why we can be so productive and prone to time blindness.

Smash The Boulder

Avoid over-loading us and keep verbal instructions to a minimum. Where possible, make requests by email or add them to a physical to-do list. If we're concentrating on something and you need to give us an additional task, writing the details on our notepad or simply adding a note for us to contact you for the details of what you want us to do, will work effectively and do much to reduce the likelihood of creating overload leading to overwhelm and venting.

Be absolutely clear in the language that you use. Remember, autists are literal thinkers. Instructions need to be clear and complete. Please don't assume that by giving half an instruction, the autist will figure out the rest of it by inference. Always say what you mean and mean what you say. No hints please, you'll only end up disappointed.

If an autist has applied for a position and declared being autistic, please let them know exactly what to expect at the interview. If your recruitment process includes expecting an applicant to speak freely about themselves rather than give responses to your questions, let them know in advance. Otherwise, you may find yourself in a silent stand-off while the autist waits for you to actually interview them (per invitation) and they won't know why you're looking at them expectantly. It would also help to provide autistic applicants with a list of the questions before the interview. This is because processing delays and memory issues make it difficult for us to produce examples of experiences quickly. It can look like we don't have any proof of our abilities when we just need more time to consider the question and relate it back to our experiences.

Please don't mock our communication style in training sessions, but make everyone aware of the differences. Let everyone know why the differences exist. Teach staff how to recognise autistic people and encourage mutual respect. Training in the workplace is the most efficient way of spreading the message and educating the wider society. Without it, there's little hope of eliminating the contempt and distrust that the autistic working community experiences on a daily basis.

Let the rest of the team know that the latest recruit is autistic. Run this by the autist first, but if they've declared it to recruitment, it's unlikely they would have an issue with their colleagues also knowing. Make sure others know what this means and what to expect and request that they ask the autist directly if there's something they want to know – avoid assumption and gossip.

If it helps, tell everyone to remember it's not personal. Bruised egos don't help anybody. Hanging on to perceived slights and misunderstandings, when the autist intended no offense, harms everybody, particularly in small working environments. Tolerance and acceptance lead to peaceful working environments; not hostility, resentment and contempt.

That said, please listen to us when we say we can't trust someone. It doesn't matter if they deny any wrongdoing because punishment isn't necessary. We just need management to be aware of what's happening and respect our need for distance. We feel vulnerable because we know we are.

Remember that we all have needs – not just neurotypicals – and nobody should think it's okay to expect to have everything their own way. Compromise is always a winner.

Thanks for Listening

I hope I've covered everything and I don't doubt I'll get feedback about anything I've forgotten! I hope the ride hasn't been too bumpy. I appreciate how hard some of what I've said would've been to swallow, but to gloss over anything would've rendered the entire exercise of writing this book pointless.

In my lifetime, misogyny has been pervasive and normal. The accepted arrogance of men as it was in the seventies has mostly gone, even if there are still areas of inequality between the sexes. The situation where homosexuality was illegal and gay people criminalised is gone. Most people recognise that skin colour shouldn't separate us. But, we have a long way to go in reaching a point where society recognises autistic traits for what they really are and where autistic people are no longer vilified for their differences.

Eliza Jane Blake

There's no equality for us in mainstream organisations, yet. The burden to compromise and fit in lies entirely on the shoulders of the very people least equipped to meet the expectations of others. And why should they? How can they? Autistic traits aren't a choice. They aren't a personality or character flaw. Those who look down their noses at us have no comprehension of how different their lives would've been if they'd been the ones born autistic.

As hard as it may be, those neurotypicals who believe they shouldn't have to accommodate us need to recognise that their life experience isn't the only one that matters. They're not the only ones with needs and rights. Nobody should have to spend their life cautiously navigating, hoping not to upset anyone unintentionally, or to become so defensive it feels like they're carrying the weight of iron-body-armour on their shoulders in their social interactions.

We've carried the burden, with no room for error, for long enough. It's time to meet us half-way. Society can't continue expecting us to be just like them while recognising us as disabled. Most of us are capable of productive work and want to work. Our biggest hindrance is ignorance, unrealistic expectations, a refusal to compromise, and in the arena of work, company policies that recommend and sanction punishing us when we don't meet neurotypical standards. Nobody can expect to have everything their own way and nobody has a right to demand that their comfort zones are never stretched. Awareness is key.

Some people believe autistic brains are of low intelligence and will produce statistics to back up their claim, but those statistics are flawed simply because the numbers they're based upon are incomplete. The growth of known autistic people continues to rise at an exponential rate and the figures are changing fast.

The organisations and systems responsible for assessing individuals are under tremendous pressure to accommodate the avalanche rolling through their doors as more and more people come to realise there may be a reason for their problems, and services are struggling to cope with the demand in a timely fashion.

Undiagnosed adults are jumping on the internet and tapping into the wealth of information that's already out there, enabling them to recognise their own plight. They're being forced to diagnose themselves because of the length of waiting time through the NHS and the prohibitive cost of seeking a private diagnosis. It's shocking that a condition that's so debilitating to most who meet the criteria for diagnosis must first be able to diagnose themselves before they can ever hope to win an audience with a professional to have their suspicions confirmed. But that's where we're at.

Autistic brains aren't becoming more prevalent in society, just more recognised. We've always been there and awareness is growing, mostly thanks to the internet. A significant minority group who've spent their lives shunned by society and forced to live 'half a life' on the outside, are now gaining access to the information that's enabling them to make sense of their lives and make their voice heard.

We've been silenced, judged and punished for too long. We deserve fair access to the job market and the chance to live productive lives. The arrogant and facetious comments that so often come our way need to stop.

Neurotypicals don't appreciate being patronised and neither do we, but we are – all the time – because people don't know they're diminishing and belittling people whose only crime has been to be born with different brain programming.

To promote inclusivity, people entering a new workplace are now being invited to bring their true selves to work. It's a broad invitation extended to all new employees, but for us, we're walking into a minefield. It was bad enough before, but if we let our guard down or take off the mask we spent a lifetime building, we're putting ourselves into the firing line for even more abuse and misunderstanding than ever. The invitation is well-intentioned, but damaging because so few understand the autistic neurotype.

Being autistic in a world that doesn't understand us and is so quick to destroy our self-esteem with shaming tactics leads to many capable and productive people being written out of the employment market altogether. Society needs to correct the prevalent wider ignorance for true inclusivity to prevail.

All the big companies are behind this initiative and make a big demonstration of their commitment to it. Besides inviting their new recruits to bring their true selves to work, some even send out questionnaires to monitor how their policy is working, asking colleagues if they feel comfortable bringing their true selves to work. While this is great for most minorities, it's not, however, where neurodivergent people are concerned.

Companies that invite neurodivergent workers to bring their true selves to work without first educating their managers, trainers and existing employees in what neurodiversity can look like, potentially expose us to more abuse than we already receive. I think the most harmful platitude I've ever heard has been the phrase to just be myself. It's the one thing we've never been able to be if we want to survive in this world.

So, thank you for taking the time to read this book. Your knowledge could make a massive difference to the life of someone who feels misunderstood and marginalised, even at their wits' end and considering suicide.

For once, I'm grateful for all the negative experiences I've survived in the workplace, because without them, writing this book wouldn't have been possible. It's time to correct the misunderstandings and reject the accepted wisdom that's passed down through the generations.

I truly hope we can come to understand and recognise different neurotypes, fostering a new era of positive working relationships where we accept neurodivergence in modern workplaces without fear, mistrust, judgement, or friction.

We all deserve better.

Acknowledgements

I'd just like to say thank you to my son for keeping me going during the past few years (although he probably doesn't realise he did). I wouldn't have made it without him.

Thank you to all the Monday Motivation gang, but especially Cole Burke, Andrew Guile, Kay Weetch and Becky Fussell for being a constant source of support since we met in January 2017.

Thank you to the Write Magic group, too. Especially to those who took part in Bootcamp during May 2024. I made a mistake when calculating my target for the month and then had to deliver on it with the Admins (they know who they are) driving me on with an iron rod and the threat of 'sadistic' punishment if I let myself down. I made a lot of progress during that fateful month!

Smash The Boulder

Finally, I'd like to thank everyone who has taken the time to read *Smash the Boulder* and I'd like to make an apology. I know only too well the value of employing the services of an editor and independent proofreader during the production of a project such as this, but I didn't. As irrational as it may sound, this book was just too personal. I didn't want any interference, even if it was well-intentioned. I wanted it to be completely authentic and honest. So, I apologise for any oversights caused by a lack of fresh eyes checking the text.

Reviews help a book's visibility. If you have time to leave a review, no matter how short, it may improve the prospects of autistic people now and in the future. Your help would be gratefully received.

I'd also welcome your thoughts on all the issues raised in this book. It's such an important conversation, I'll be producing a Feedback on Feedback newsletter. If you'd like to contribute, please email me:

eliza@awesomescribblersunited.uk

All who contribute will receive a copy of the newsletter.

Thank you.

About the Author

With a lifelong passion for books, stories, and the written word, I'm a writer and qualified proofreader. I trained with the Chartered Institute of Editors and Proofreaders and remain a member with a desire to gain the work experience required to progress through the levels of membership. I'm also a qualified bookkeeper with a history of working in accounts, credit control and admin. In the past, I qualified as a hypnotherapist (hypnotist in the US) and, while I never practiced, I have an enduring interest in psychology and enjoy helping others. I also worked in the community care industry for twelve years.

In 2018, the direction of my life changed unexpectedly. No great trauma occurred, but my life took an unexpected turn when a curtain that had cast a shadow over my life until that point pulled back slightly, allowing a pinprick of light to break through. It was then that I realised I might be autistic. After conducting several months of research, I embarked on the journey to diagnosis in 2019.

Smash The Boulder

Three years after the initial assessment, I received confirmation of my diagnosis. It had been a long and frustrating road, but finally, my life experience made some sense. What really baffled me was how an autistic adult could live for so long without their difference being realised. Surely someone must have known!

In my case, the reason was frighteningly simple. I'd always enjoyed learning and therefore, school hadn't been a problem. Recognition of neurodivergence in children has improved in recent years, but for my generation, teachers only noticed us if we were disruptive or falling behind and even then, it was unlikely they would know why. I was neither struggling academically nor causing problems in the classroom, but because of the lack of diagnosis and subsequent lack of help or support in a social sense, my complimentary and positive school reports made no difference to my life after school.

From the start, I received odd looks from other people and found myself on the receiving end of spiteful behaviour without knowing why. Worse than that, I always felt that I was living my life with one arm tied behind my back; that people were actively stopping me from progressing at work just because they didn't like me.

Three years is a painfully long time to be forced to wait for a diagnosis when the reason for your struggles hasn't only had a tremendous impact on your life, but continues to do so. It does, however, reflect the exponential demand for assessments in a society that's slowly awakening to the reality of other types of brain function and mental processing. For me, the wait was worth it. I'm proud to be a detail-driven autist and my writing projects now focus upon raising autistic awareness and acceptance of this greatly misunderstood neurotype.

Discrimination exists in many forms, and for most minority groups, is already being addressed. But for autists, however, this isn't the case. People like me are gaining some traction in bringing an awareness of our reality to the rest of the world, but without understanding, there can be no tolerance and without tolerance, there can be no acceptance.

The lack of awareness in relation to the breadth of the Spectrum leads many people to believe that *all* autistic people can't exist without significant support. When in truth, many autistic people don't appear disabled at all, but that doesn't mean they're not struggling. Rather, they're creating a long-term challenge for themselves by masking excessively, or people assume they're bad neurotypicals and punish them instead of offering support.

This is a situation that desperately needs to change and is the reason I wrote *Smash the Boulder*. I'm hoping to improve relationships in the workplace and enable those autistic people who're struggling to be granted the chance of a better life.

awesomescribblersunited.com

eliza@awesomescribblersunited.uk

Awesome Scribblers United and its associated logo are trademarked in the United Kingdom

www.ingramcontent.com/pod-product-compliance
Lightning Source LLC
Chambersburg PA
CBHW030436010526
44118CB00011B/668